JAMESTOWN EDUCATION

FUSION READING Plus

Introductory

Mc Graw Hill Education

Bothell, WA • Chicago, IL • Columbus, OH • New York, NY

www.mheonline.com

The *McGraw·Hill* Companies

Education

Send all inquiries to:
McGraw-Hill Education
130 E. Randolph, Suite 400
Chicago, IL 60601

ISBN: 978-0-07-662720-2
MHID: 0-07-662720-9
Printed in the United States of America.

2 3 4 5 6 7 8 9 QFR 16 15 14 13 12

Contents

To the Student

You probably speak at a rate of about 150 words per minute. If you are a reader of average ability, you read at a rate of about 250 words per minute. So your reading speed is nearly twice as fast as your speaking or listening speed. This example shows that reading is one of the fastest ways to get information.

About This Book

The purpose of this book is to help you increase your reading rate and understand what you read. The 54 lessons in this book will also give you practice in reading informational articles and in preparing for tests in which you must read and understand nonfiction passages within a certain time limit.

Reading Faster and Better

The following are some strategies that you can use to read the articles in each lesson.

Previewing

When you read, do you start with the first word, or do you look over the whole selection for a moment? Previewing before you read is a very important step. This helps you to get an idea of what a selection is about and to recall any previous knowledge you have about the subject. Here are the steps to follow when previewing.

Read the title. Titles are designed not only to announce the subject but also to make the reader think. Ask yourself questions such as What can I learn from the title? What thoughts does it bring to mind? What do I already know about this subject?

Read the first sentence. If they are short, read the first two sentences. The opening sentence is the writer's opportunity to get your attention. Some writers announce what they hope to tell you in the selection. Some writers state their purpose for writing; others just try to get your attention.

Read the last sentence. If they are short, read the final two sentences. The closing sentence is the writer's last chance to get ideas across to you. Some writers repeat the main idea once more. Some writers draw a conclusion—this is what they have been leading up to. Other writers summarize their thoughts; they tie all the facts together.

Skim the entire selection. Glance through the selection quickly to see what other information you can pick up. Look for anything that will help you read fluently and with understanding. Are there names, dates, or numbers? If so, you may have to read more slowly.

Reading for Meaning

When you read, do you just see words? Are you so occupied with reading words that you sometimes fail to get their meaning? Here are some ways to make sure you are making sense of what you read.

Build your concentration. You cannot understand what you read if you are not concentrating. When you discover that your thoughts are straying, correct the situation right away. Avoid distractions and distracting situations. Keep in mind the information you learned from previewing. This will help focus your attention on the selection.

Read in thought groups. Try to see words in meaningful combinations—phrases, clauses, or sentences. If you look only at one word at a time (called word-by-word reading), both your comprehension and your reading speed suffer.

Ask yourself questions. To sustain the pace you have set for yourself and to maintain a high level of concentration and comprehension, ask yourself questions such as What does this mean? or How can I use this information? as you read.

Finding the Main Ideas

The paragraph is the basic unit of meaning. If you can quickly discover and understand the main idea of each paragraph, you will build your comprehension of the selection. Good readers know how to find main ideas quickly. This helps make them faster readers.

Find the topic sentence. The topic sentence, which contains the main idea, is often the first sentence of a paragraph. It is followed by sentences that support, develop, or explain the main idea. Sometimes a topic sentence comes at the end of a paragraph. When it does, the supporting details come first, building the base for the topic sentence. Some paragraphs do not have a topic sentence; all of the sentences combine to create a meaningful idea.

Understand paragraph structure. Every well-written paragraph has a purpose. The purpose may be to inform, define, explain, illustrate, and so on. The purpose should always relate to the main idea and expand on it. As you read each paragraph, see how the body of the paragraph tells you more about the main idea.

Organizing the Facts

When you read, do you tend to learn a lot of facts without any apparent connection or relationship? Understanding how the facts all fit together to deliver information is, after all, the reason for reading. Good readers organize facts as they read. This helps them read rapidly and well.

Determine the writer's purpose. Every writer has a plan or outline to follow. If you can discover the writer's method of organization, you have a key to understanding the selection. Sometimes there are obvious signals. The statement "There are three reasons . . ." should prompt you to look for a listing of three items. Other less obvious signal words such as *moreover, otherwise,* and *consequently* help you decide how to process the information.

Relate ideas as you read. As you read the selection, keep in mind the information you learned from previewing. See how the writer is attempting to piece together ideas. As you discover the relationship among the ideas, the main ideas come through quickly and clearly.

Mastering Reading Comprehension

Reading fast is not useful if you don't remember or understand what you read. The reading-comprehension exercise provides a check on how well you have understood the article.

Recalling Facts

These multiple-choice questions provide a quick check to see how well you recall important information from the article. As you learn to apply the reading strategies described above, you should be able to answer these questions more successfully.

Understanding Ideas

These questions require you to think about the main ideas in the article. Some of these ideas are stated in the article; others are not. To answer some of the questions, you need to draw conclusions about what you read.

Working Through Each Lesson

1. **Preview the article.** Locate the timed selection of the lesson that you are going to read. Wait for your teacher's signal to preview. You will have 20 seconds for previewing. Follow the previewing steps that begin on page i.

2. **Read the article.** When your teacher gives you the signal, begin reading. Read carefully so that you will be able to answer questions about what you have read. When you finish reading, look at the board and note your reading time. Write this time at the bottom of the page on the line labeled Reading Time.

3. **Complete the exercises.** Answer the 10 questions that follow the article. There are five fact questions and five idea questions. Choose the best answer to each question and put an X in that box.

4. **Correct your work.** Use the Answer Key at the back of the book to check your answers. Circle any wrong answer and put an X in the box you should have marked. Record the number of correct answers on the appropriate line at the end of the lesson.

Plotting Your Progress

Find your reading rate. Turn to the Reading Rate graph that follows each unit. Put an X at the point where the vertical line that represents the lesson intersects your reading time, shown along the left-hand side. The right-hand side of the graph will reveal your words-per-minute reading speed. Your teacher will review this graph from time to time to evaluate your progress.

Find your comprehension score. Determine your total number of correct answers and record that number on the appropriate line. Turn to the Comprehension Score graph that follows each unit. Put an X at the point where the vertical line that represents your lesson intersects your total correct answers, shown along the left-hand side. The right-hand side of the graph will show the percentage of questions you answered correctly.

To get the most benefit from these lessons, you need to take charge of your own progress in improving your reading speed and comprehension. Studying these graphs will help you to see whether your skills are improving and to determine what skills you need to work on. Your teacher will also want to review the graphs to see how your reading rate is progressing and to detect any comprehension problems you may be experiencing. Your achievement, as shown on both of the graphs, will determine your readiness to move on to higher and more challenging levels.

To the Teacher

About the Fusion Reading Plus Series

Fusion Reading Plus consists of three books with reading levels that range from 5–13. Each book contains three units, each of which has 18 articles at a prescribed reading level. The Introductory level contains material at reading levels 5–7; the Intermediate level at reading levels 8–10; and the Advanced level at reading levels 11–13. The reading levels are determined by the Lexile Framework for Reading and are not to be confused with grade or age levels. The books are designed for use with students at middle school level and above.

The purposes of the series are as follows:

- to provide systematic, structured reading practice that helps students improve their reading rate and comprehension skills

- to give students practice in reading and understanding informational articles

- to prepare students for taking standardized tests that include timed reading passages

- to provide materials with a wide range of reading levels so that students can continue to practice and improve their reading rate and comprehension skills

The topics in this series are not correlated to any grade-level curriculum because the books are designed for use with students at designated reading levels rather than in a particular grade. Most standardized tests require students to read and comprehend passages.

About the Books

Each book in the series contains 54 lessons. Each lesson focuses on improving reading rate. These lessons consist of a 400-word timed informational article on a topic followed by a multiple-choice reading-comprehension exercise. Recalling Facts includes five fact questions; Understanding Ideas includes five critical thinking questions.

Timed Reading and Comprehension

Timed reading is the best-known method of improving reading speed. There is no point in someone reading at an accelerated speed if the person does not understand what she or he is reading. There is nothing more important than comprehension in reading: the main purpose of reading is to gain knowledge and insight; to understand the information that the writer and the text are communicating.

Very few students will be able to read a passage once and answer all of the questions correctly. Usually a score of 70 or 80 percent correct is relatively normal. If the student gets 90 or 100 percent correct, he or she is probably either reading too slowly or the material is at too low a reading level. A comprehension or critical thinking score below 70 percent indicates a need for improvement.

One method of improving comprehension and critical thinking skills is for the student to go back and study each question answered incorrectly. First, the question should be read again very carefully. It is surprising how many students get the wrong answer simply because they have not read the question carefully. After doing this, the student should look back in the selection to find the place where the question is answered, reread that part of the selection, and think about how to arrive at the correct answer. It is important to be able to recognize a correct answer when it is embedded in the text. Teacher guidance or class discussion will help a student find an answer.

Speed Versus Comprehension

It is not unusual for students' comprehension scores to decline as their reading rate increases during the early weeks of timed readings. If this happens, the student should attempt to level off his or her speed—but not lower it—and concentrate more on comprehension. Usually, if the student maintains the higher speed and concentrates on comprehension, scores will gradually improve and within a week or two return to normal levels of 70 to 80 percent.

Achieving a proper balance between speed and comprehension is one of the most important things to learn. An inefficient reader typically reads everything at one speed, usually slowly. Some poor readers, however, read rapidly, but without satisfactory comprehension. The important thing is to achieve a balance between speed and comprehension. The practice this series provides enables students to increase their reading speed while maintaining normal levels of comprehension.

Getting Started

As a rule, the passages in a book designed to improve reading speed should be relatively easy for the student. The student should not have much difficulty with the vocabulary or the subject matter. Don't worry about the passages being too easy; students should see how quickly and efficiently they can read a passage.

Begin by assigning students to a level. A student should start with a book that is one level below his or her current reading level. If a student's reading level is not known, a suitable starting point would be one or two levels below the student's present grade in school.

Timing the Reading

One suggestion for timing the reading is to have all students begin reading the selection at the same time. Use a stopwatch or an interactive whiteboard timer to keep track of the time. After one minute, indicate that the time has elapsed and begin updating it at 10-second intervals (1:00, 1:10, 1:20, etc.).

How to Use the Books

Introduce students to the contents and format of the book you are using. Examine the book to see how it is set up. Talk about the parts of each lesson. Discuss the purpose of timed reading and the use of the progress graphs at the end of each unit.

Teaching a Lesson

1. Give students the signal to begin previewing the lesson. Allow 20 seconds for this. Pause to discuss any special terms or vocabulary that students have found in their previewing.

2. Use one of the methods described above to time students as they read the passage. (Include the 20-second preview time as part of the first minute.) Tell students to write down the last time shown on the board or stopwatch when they finish reading. Have them record the time in the designated space after the passage and on the Reading Rate graph that follows each unit.

3. Next, have students complete the reading-comprehension exercise by marking the correct answers with an X. Work with them to check their answers using the Answer Key that begins on page 115. Have them circle incorrect answers and then record their scores on the appropriate line at the end of the lesson. Correct responses to eight or more questions indicate satisfactory comprehension and recall.

Monitoring Progress

Scoring

Have students find their total correct answers and record them on the Comprehension Score graphs at the end of each unit.

Using the Graphs

Reading times are plotted on the Reading Rate graph that follows each unit. The legend on the graph automatically converts reading times to words-per-minute rates. Comprehension totals are plotted on the Comprehension Score graph. Plotting automatically converts the raw scores to a comprehension percentage based on 10 points per correct answer.

These graphs provide a visual record of a student's progress. This record gives the student and the teacher an opportunity to evaluate the student's progress and determine what types of exercises and skills she or he needs to concentrate on.

Diagnosis and Evaluation

The following are typical reading rates.

Slow Reader—150 words per minute

Average Reader—250 words per minute

Fast Reader—350 words per minute

A student who consistently reads at an average or above rate (with satisfactory comprehension) is ready to advance to the next level in the series. Before moving on to the next level, students should be encouraged to maintain their speed and comprehension by completing several additional lessons.

Birds of the Air

Almost all animals that fly belong to two groups, one without and the other with backbones. In the days of the dinosaurs, the birds had backboned rivals in the air. There were many flying reptiles. But times have changed. Birds now outnumber several hundred to one the other vertebrates (those with backbones) that can fly.

Just as there are a few flying vertebrates that are not birds, there are some birds that cannot fly. Since the time when birds were new on the Earth, there have been some flightless birds. Among the flightless birds of today are the ostriches and kiwis. Most birds, however, can fly at least a short distance. Many are remarkable flyers—they fly both fast and for long distances.

Scientists have timed some birds to find out exactly how fast they can fly. The robin's speed is about 30 miles (48 kilometers) per hour. The chimney swift can fly more than twice as fast.

Wings are needed for real flight. A flying fish can soar through the air for a little way. A flying squirrel can glide from one branch to another. But only creatures with true wings can really fly.

A typical bird's wings are powered by strong wing muscles. On the breastbone, there is a projection called a keel to which the wing muscles are fastened. As it flies, a bird beats its wings against the air and pushes itself forward.

A bird's light weight is a help in flying. A chimney swift weighs less than a mouse or toad of the same size. One reason a bird is so light is because many of its bones are hollow. They are filled with air. Connected with its lungs, a bird also has tiny air sacs throughout its body. These tiny air sacs act like little hot-air balloons.

Many birds use their power of flying to spend their winters in one part of the world and their summers in another. In the northern part of the United States, the appearance of robins is one of the first signs of spring. The robin goes south in the fall and returns in early spring. The chimney swift is a traveler, too. It leaves earlier than the robin in the fall, comes back later in the spring, and travels farther.

Not all birds travel. Some live in one region all their lives.

Reading Time _____

Recalling Facts

1. Birds are
   - ☐ a. vertebrates.
   - ☐ b. animals without backbones.
   - ☐ c. flying reptiles.

2. To really fly, creatures need
   - ☐ a. feathers.
   - ☐ b. real wings.
   - ☐ c. long tails.

3. Many of a bird's bones are
   - ☐ a. filled with water.
   - ☐ b. hollow.
   - ☐ c. like tiny hot-air balloons.

4. A bird's wing muscles are fastened to
   - ☐ a. a bone on its back.
   - ☐ b. each side.
   - ☐ c. a keel on its breastbone.

5. A bird that flies twice as fast as a robin is the
   - ☐ a. kiwi.
   - ☐ b. canary.
   - ☐ c. chimney swift.

Understanding Ideas

6. You can conclude from the article that vertebrates that fly
   - ☐ a. include birds and other animals.
   - ☐ b. are all birds.
   - ☐ c. are mostly animals other than birds.

7. It is likely that the smaller a bird is,
   - ☐ a. the faster it can fly.
   - ☐ b. the more hollow bones it has.
   - ☐ c. the lighter it is.

8. Compared to a mammal of the same size, a bird probably weighs
   - ☐ a. about the same.
   - ☐ b. more.
   - ☐ c. less.

9. It is likely that robins fly south in order to
   - ☐ a. get exercise.
   - ☐ b. avoid cold weather.
   - ☐ c. mate.

10. You can conclude that the speed at which different birds fly
    - ☐ a. is about the same.
    - ☐ b. varies from bird to bird.
    - ☐ c. depends mostly on the weather.

Correct Answers _____

Sleeping Through the Winter

To survive, animals learn how to adjust to changes in their world. Some have learned how to live through cold winters when food is in short supply. Their secret is a winter sleep called hibernation. When temperatures drop, these animals go to sleep.

The best-known hibernator is the bear. All bears can hibernate. But mainly it is those that live in colder climates that do.

Before bears settle down for a long winter sleep, they stuff themselves with food. Bears eat many kinds of food including fish. But one of their favorite foods is honey. They will do almost anything to get it. They also like berries. Berries help a bear put on the extra fat it needs for its long winter sleep. In the late summer and early fall, ripe berries are plentiful. Hungry bears eat as many berries as they can find. Some bears may even travel as much as 100 miles (160 kilometers) to feast on berries.

It is true that bears hibernate during the winter because food is scarce. Yet, they have another reason to take to the den during the cold months. This is when their cubs are born. Bear cubs are usually born two to a litter. At birth, they are very tiny compared to their mother. She may weigh as much as 600 to 800 pounds (270 to 360 kilograms). Her cubs may weigh less than a pound (one-half kilogram) apiece. The cubs are blind and helpless during the first few weeks after birth. In this state, they could never survive the harsh cold. The winter den keeps the cubs safe and warm.

Bears' winter dens vary with the kind of bear that uses them and the climate of the area. The dens of smaller bears may be little more than a hollow stump. Some dens are just holes dug in a riverbank. Larger bears, however, need bigger dens. Grizzlies, for example, dig out a den that is 10 to 12 feet (3 to 3.5 meters) deep. They bed it down with leaves. Then they seal it with earth and stones. Some bears in Yellowstone National Park even enjoy steam-heated caves among the hot springs. Black bears often build a den under a thick pile of logs. Or they may choose the roots of an upturned tree and let the heavy winter snows provide a good roof. Hibernating keeps bears safe and sound.

Reading Time _____

Recalling Facts

1. Animals hibernate because
   - ☐ a. they don't like cold weather.
   - ☐ b. food is scarce.
   - ☐ c. they need rest.

2. Berries are ripe during
   - ☐ a. early fall.
   - ☐ b. the late winter.
   - ☐ c. early summer.

3. Bears usually give birth to
   - ☐ a. one cub.
   - ☐ b. two cubs.
   - ☐ c. three cubs.

4. Bears' dens vary with the kind of bear and the
   - ☐ a. climate.
   - ☐ b. time of year.
   - ☐ c. number of cubs that are born.

5. Black bears often build dens in
   - ☐ a. hollow stumps.
   - ☐ b. thick piles of logs.
   - ☐ c. earth and stones.

Understanding Ideas

6. You can conclude from the article that in cold climates
   - ☐ a. all animals hibernate.
   - ☐ b. only bears hibernate.
   - ☐ c. some animals hibernate.

7. Hibernation is one way that animals have learned to
   - ☐ a. find needed food.
   - ☐ b. sleep better.
   - ☐ c. adjust to their surroundings.

8. If bears did not hibernate, their cubs would most likely
   - ☐ a. starve.
   - ☐ b. die from the cold.
   - ☐ c. get lost.

9. Bears that live in warm climates
   - ☐ a. hibernate during the summer.
   - ☐ b. travel north to hibernate.
   - ☐ c. do not need to hibernate.

10. You can conclude from the article that bears
    - ☐ a. are plant eaters.
    - ☐ b. are meat eaters.
    - ☐ c. eat meat and plants.

Correct Answers _____

FUSION Reading *Plus*

Swim Safely

Swimming is enjoyed by people of all ages, from the very young to the very old. All over the world people swim for fun. There are many places where people can enjoy swimming. People swim in lakes, oceans, and rivers. Some swim in pools. Many schools, motels, apartment buildings, and clubs have indoor or outdoor pools. Some families have pools in their yards.

Swimming is one of the best forms of exercise. It can improve heart function and it helps blood circulate. Swimming develops strong muscles. It will even strengthen the lungs. People who are disabled and can't enjoy other sports can keep their bodies in better condition by swimming.

It is a good idea for parents to make sure that their children learn to swim at an early age. This will be an activity that the children can enjoy for the rest of their lives.

There are basic rules for water safety that can help save your life. These rules can also help you save the life of a friend.

First of all, know how to swim. Many schools give lessons to children as part of their athletic program. Adults can learn to swim at public pools or recreation centers.

Another rule to remember is never swim alone. Always swim with a friend and know where that person is in the water at all times. It is best to swim only in places where there is a lifeguard, but if you swim in the ocean or a river, it is good to know about tides and currents.

Whether you are a beginner or an experienced swimmer, it is good to know survival bobbing as this can help you if there is an accident. Survival bobbing lets you float for a long time on your stomach. This bobbing uses very little energy. You fill your lungs with air, and at the same time, you relax your body. Your arms and legs hang down limply, and your chin lowers to your chest. The air in your lungs will hold your head above the water. When you need a breath, you breathe out through your nose. Then you lift your face out of the water and breathe in through your mouth. You then return to the restful floating position.

Never take dangerous chances when swimming. Most drownings could be avoided if everyone knew how to swim and followed the basic rules for water safety.

Reading Time _____

Recalling Facts

1. Swimming can help improve
   - ☐ a. heart action.
   - ☐ b. eyesight.
   - ☐ c. hearing.

2. An important rule in swimming is
   - ☐ a. swim in deep water.
   - ☐ b. never swim alone.
   - ☐ c. always float.

3. Survival bobbing means
   - ☐ a. floating on your back.
   - ☐ b. pushing up and down with your legs.
   - ☐ c. floating on your stomach.

4. It is best to swim in
   - ☐ a. swimming pools.
   - ☐ b. places where there is a lifeguard.
   - ☐ c. lakes.

5. Swimming can help develop
   - ☐ a. strong muscles.
   - ☐ b. memory.
   - ☐ c. creative ability.

Understanding Ideas

6. The more air in your lungs, the more
   - ☐ a. you will sink.
   - ☐ b. you will float.
   - ☐ c. your body will weigh.

7. Survival bobbing should be learned
   - ☐ a. by anyone who swims.
   - ☐ b. by beginner swimmers only.
   - ☐ c. only as a last resort.

8. You can conclude from the article that the best way to avoid drowning is to
   - ☐ a. swim in pools.
   - ☐ b. swim in shallow water.
   - ☐ c. follow the basic rules for water safety.

9. The article suggests that swimming is
   - ☐ a. beneficial for most people.
   - ☐ b. a dangerous sport.
   - ☐ c. life-threatening.

10. You can conclude that teaching children to swim at an early age
    - ☐ a. helps save lives.
    - ☐ b. teaches good moral values.
    - ☐ c. is bad for their health.

Correct Answers _____

Bows and Arrows

4

Early people hunted with the bow more than 8,000 years ago. Bows and arrows are one of humans' oldest weapons. They were an important discovery for people. It gave them a deadly weapon with which they could kill prey from a distance. Arrows could also be used against their enemies.

The ordinary bow, or short bow, was used by nearly all early people. This bow had limited power and a short range. However, early hunters overcame these faults by learning to track their prey at close range. In fact, some African pygmies still hunt this way. They get very close to their prey and then shoot it with poisoned arrows. Moreover, North American Indians rarely tried a shot more than 40 yards (about 37 meters) away.

The longbow was most likely invented when someone found out that a five-foot (1.5-meter) piece of wood made a better bow than a three-foot (0.9-meter) piece. The final length of the longbow was probably six feet, six inches (about 2 meters). Hundreds of thousands of these bows were made and used for 300 years. However, not one is known to have survived until today. A force of about 100 pounds (45 kilograms) was needed to pull the string of the longbow all the way back. Anyone who used this bow had to be extremely strong.

The English longbow arrows were made of oak, ash, or birch. The arrows were usually feathered with wing feathers from the gray goose. The arrowheads were made of steel, and they were constructed to be broad and barbed. The archer carried 24 such arrows into battle. Archers could shoot one every five seconds if they had to. This made them a fearful enemy.

For a long time, the bow was just a bent stick and a string. In fact, more changes have taken place to the bow and arrow in the past 25 years than in the last seven centuries. Today's bow is forceful. It is as exact as a gun. Plus, little strength is needed to draw the string. Modern bows also have fine sights. An expert can hit a bull's-eye many times in a row from a good distance away. In indoor contests, perfect scores from 40 yards (about 37 meters) are common. Matches have been lost when a winning arrow was stopped by one already in the bull's-eye.

The invention of the bow ranks with the discovery of fire and the wheel. It was a great step forward for humans.

Reading Time _____

Recalling Facts

1. Nearly all early people hunted with
   - ☐ a. slingshots.
   - ☐ b. nets.
   - ☐ c. short bows.

2. The length of the longbow is estimated at about
   - ☐ a. three feet (0.9 meters).
   - ☐ b. six and a half feet (about 2 meters).
   - ☐ c. 10 feet (3 meters).

3. The longbow's main disadvantage was
   - ☐ a. the strength required to use it.
   - ☐ b. that it did not survive.
   - ☐ c. that it did not shoot straight.

4. Most of the changes to the bow and arrow were made
   - ☐ a. in the last 25 years.
   - ☐ b. 100 years ago.
   - ☐ c. centuries ago.

5. Indoor bow-and-arrow contests are won by hitting
   - ☐ a. the outer edge of the target.
   - ☐ b. the bull's-eye.
   - ☐ c. objects tossed in the air.

Understanding Ideas

6. Bows probably came about as a result of
   - ☐ a. scientific experimentation.
   - ☐ b. a lack of gunpowder.
   - ☐ c. trial and error.

7. It is likely that American Indians did not try to use a short bow to shoot arrows past forty yards because
   - ☐ a. they were poor shots.
   - ☐ b. the bow was not accurate at greater distances.
   - ☐ c. they were not strong enough.

8. You can conclude from the article that longer bows are generally
   - ☐ a. more accurate than shorter bows.
   - ☐ b. more difficult to use than shorter bows.
   - ☐ c. more expensive than shorter bows.

9. The short bow and longbow most likely get their names from
   - ☐ a. the range of the bow.
   - ☐ b. the height of the person using the weapon.
   - ☐ c. the length of the bow.

10. You can conclude that the invention of the bow is considered
    - ☐ a. an invention of great importance.
    - ☐ b. the greatest invention in history.
    - ☐ c. more important than the invention of the wheel or fire.

Correct Answers _____

Life of a Logger

5

Early loggers led an unsettled life, wandering from one job to another. Many stayed at a logging camp for only a few days or weeks. Their work was hard and long. They were free only on Sundays and evenings. Loggers worked 11 hours a day until their workday was reduced to 10 hours in 1910. After 1920, loggers worked eight hours a day, five days a week. Usually they worked even in rain, snow, and freezing cold. If bad weather did stop work, they were not paid for lost time.

A typical logging camp contained a bunkhouse, a cookhouse, a dining room, and an office. There were stables and a blacksmith's shop and perhaps a store, a meat house, and storage sheds. The number of buildings depended on the number of workers and on the kind of equipment to be stored and maintained.

The bunkhouses were rude buildings that had tiers of bunks nailed to the walls. There was just room enough between a bunk and the one above it for a worker to crawl into bed and roll over. Often double bunks were used. One worker would be assigned to each side. Blankets and sometimes a straw mattress were furnished. Otherwise the workers made do with spruce boughs. Bedbugs were a common complaint. A stove in the middle of the room provided heat. After working in the rain or snow or doing their laundry, the loggers hung their clothes around the stove to dry. The smoke from the stove mixed with the steam from the wet clothes.

The day began at 5:00 a.m. when the bull cook (the camp odd-jobs worker) woke the loggers. At 5:30 a.m., the gong sounded for the huge breakfast that prepared them for the day's work. The cook was one of the most important and best-paid workers in the camp. The meals made had to satisfy the ravenous appetites of the hardworking loggers. If they did not like their food, they might refuse to work.

At 9:00 p.m., the lights were turned out. The workers immediately went to bed and were quiet. They needed plenty of rest just as they needed plenty of food.

Loggers whose homes were near the camp could leave it on Saturday evening and return on Sunday. The others could not leave until payday. Most evenings were spent playing cards or spinning yarns (telling made-up stories). Many legends grew out of these loggers' tales.

Reading Time _____

Recalling Facts

1. An early logger's workday lasted
   ☐ a. nine hours.
   ☐ b. 11 hours.
   ☐ c. 15 hours.

2. Loggers slept in
   ☐ a. stables.
   ☐ b. tents.
   ☐ c. bunkhouses.

3. A logger's workday began at
   ☐ a. 3:00 a.m.
   ☐ b. 5:00 a.m.
   ☐ c. 9:00 a.m.

4. The job of a bull cook in a logging camp was to
   ☐ a. perform odd jobs.
   ☐ b. slaughter bulls for cooking.
   ☐ c. cook breakfast.

5. The loggers' workday was reduced to eight hours in
   ☐ a. the 1800s.
   ☐ b. 1910.
   ☐ c. the 1920s.

Understanding Ideas

6. It is likely that early loggers
   ☐ a. were envied for their jobs.
   ☐ b. were well paid.
   ☐ c. received low wages.

7. You can conclude from the article that conditions in logging camps today
   ☐ a. have changed little from the early days.
   ☐ b. have improved over those of the early days.
   ☐ c. are worse than in the early days.

8. You can conclude that a typical logging camp included
   ☐ a. horses.
   ☐ b. cars.
   ☐ c. bicycles.

9. It is likely that loggers' yarns came from
   ☐ a. books they had read.
   ☐ b. their imaginations.
   ☐ c. historical events.

10. Logging camps were most likely located
    ☐ a. in forested areas.
    ☐ b. by the ocean.
    ☐ c. in areas with warm climates.

Correct Answers _____

The Need for Clean Water

People have come to realize how important water is. All animals and plants are mostly water. A person's body is about 65 percent water. People need to drink at least five pints (2.4 liters) of water each day. Large animals need about 15 gallons (57 liters) of water a day. Water has other uses, too. It is used for washing and air conditioning in addition to household work and gardening. Steel, gasoline, paper, and most other products are made with the help of water. Power plants use water for cooling. Farms, of course, need water to grow food.

Water is used by industries to transport goods and by people to travel around the world. Water is used for swimming, boating, and other kinds of recreation. Water is the home of many animals and plants, such as fish, whales, clams, and seaweeds. It is easy to see that life would be impossible without water. That is why it is so important to keep Earth's water clean and usable. Yet, polluted water is becoming very common.

Water that has become polluted is unsafe to use. Pollution can happen when sewage and other untreated wastes have been dumped into the water. Polluted water can smell, have garbage floating in it, and be unfit for swimming or boating. But even water that looks clean and smells good can be polluted. It may be filled with microorganisms and dangerous chemicals that cannot be seen.

People pollute water in many ways. One way is to allow bathroom and factory wastes to flow through pipes and into waterways without being treated. Another way is to allow soil, fertilizers, and industrial wastes to wash from farms, building sites, and mining sites into waterways after a rain.

Bacteria can feed on some wastes. Other wastes can be diluted by water in waterways. But nature can only do so much. People are making more waste than nature can handle. More and better wastewater treatment is needed.

It is a fact that not all towns properly treat their drinking water. Many people think that the water they drink is safe. Most of the time it is, however, about 4,000 Americans become sick each year from unsafe drinking water. Many more cases are not reported.

Clean water is so important to people's lives, and they should make an effort to ensure they will always have enough of it for now and forever.

Reading Time _____

Recalling Facts

1. People should drink at least
   - ☐ a. one pint (about .5 liters) of water a day.
   - ☐ b. five pints (2.4 liters) of water a day.
   - ☐ c. 10 pints (4.7 liters) of water a day.

2. A person's body is mostly made of
   - ☐ a. bone.
   - ☐ b. skin.
   - ☐ c. water.

3. Without water, life would be
   - ☐ a. easier.
   - ☐ b. difficult.
   - ☐ c. impossible.

4. One cause of water pollution is
   - ☐ a. dumping sewage into waterways.
   - ☐ b. rain.
   - ☐ c. using water in air conditioning.

5. Thousands of Americans become sick each year from drinking
   - ☐ a. too little water.
   - ☐ b. too much water.
   - ☐ c. unsafe water.

Understanding Ideas

6. Water that looks and smells clean
   - ☐ a. is probably safe to drink.
   - ☐ b. may be polluted.
   - ☐ c. most likely contains dangerous chemicals.

7. The article suggests that water pollution is
   - ☐ a. a growing problem.
   - ☐ b. nothing to worry about.
   - ☐ c. a problem found mostly in farming areas.

8. The main cause of water pollution is
   - ☐ a. people.
   - ☐ b. animals.
   - ☐ c. nature.

9. The article suggests that water pollution
   - ☐ a. cannot be corrected.
   - ☐ b. can be corrected by nature.
   - ☐ c. can be corrected by people.

10. You can conclude from the article that the most effective way to end water pollution is to
    - ☐ a. treat drinking water.
    - ☐ b. treat wastewater.
    - ☐ c. ban swimming and boating.

Correct Answers _____

Whitney's Cotton Gin

Eli Whitney was born just before the American Revolution. He grew up on a farm in New England. There, he showed an early ability to repair and make things. As a youth, he helped repair farm tools. He also learned how to make his own nails. At the time, Americans were still purchasing all nails from England, and they were very expensive. Once Whitney learned to make nails, he provided his father with all the nails he needed and also sold them to other people.

Whitney attended Yale University, earning his way partly by repairing tools and furniture. He also made shelves, chests, and tables for other students and professors. After graduation, he accepted a teaching position in Savannah, Georgia, a port city in the cotton-growing South.

Traveling by boat to Georgia, Whitney met Mrs. Nathaniel Greene. She was a widow of a Revolutionary War general and owned a plantation. She liked the young man and took an interest in him. When Whitney arrived in Savannah, he learned that his teaching position was no longer available. He found himself without a job and without money.

Mrs. Greene heard of Whitney's troubles, and she asked him to stay on her plantation. To thank her, he began to make things for her household— things that saved work or were convenient.

At that time, cotton was a major crop in the South. Farmers could grow great amounts of cotton. But they could not easily prepare it for market. Cotton seeds had to be removed from the cotton lint by hand. This was very slow work. Textile mills wanted more cotton. The plantation owners could grow it, but they couldn't get the cotton separated from the seeds in large enough quantities to meet demand. They were looking for a way to separate the seeds from the cotton lint more quickly.

Mrs. Greene introduced Whitney to the growers. She thought that he might be able to solve their problem. In just a few short weeks, Whitney built a simple, hand-operated machine that could separate cotton seeds from the lint. The machine could clean many more pounds (kilograms) of lint in a day than a person could by hand. Whitney's invention was the first cotton gin.

Today, thanks to machine-ginning, there is practically no limit to the amount of cotton that can be produced for factory spindles and looms. The growing of cotton has become a huge industry.

Reading Time _____

Recalling Facts

1. Eli Whitney grew up
   - ☐ a. on a southern plantation.
   - ☐ b. on a New England farm.
   - ☐ c. in Savannah, Georgia.

2. Whitney earned his way through Yale by
   - ☐ a. working as a farm laborer.
   - ☐ b. working on a boat.
   - ☐ c. repairing and making furniture.

3. Whitney accepted a teaching position
   - ☐ a. in New England.
   - ☐ b. at Yale.
   - ☐ c. in Savannah, Georgia.

4. Whitney best helped southern plantation owners by making
   - ☐ a. nails.
   - ☐ b. the cotton gin.
   - ☐ c. furniture.

5. The cotton gin
   - ☐ a. helped cotton grow faster.
   - ☐ b. separated cotton from the seeds.
   - ☐ c. made cotton into cloth.

Understanding Ideas

6. A good word to describe Eli Whitney is
   - ☐ a. carefree.
   - ☐ b. shiftless.
   - ☐ c. creative.

7. It is likely that the cotton gin was
   - ☐ a. Whitney's only invention.
   - ☐ b. one of Whitney's most important inventions.
   - ☐ c. one of Whitney's least needed inventions.

8. You can conclude from the article that after the cotton gin was invented,
   - ☐ a. plantation owners grew more cotton.
   - ☐ b. cotton became a major crop in the North.
   - ☐ c. there was less need for cotton.

9. You can conclude that textile mills
   - ☐ a. grow cotton.
   - ☐ b. no longer want cotton.
   - ☐ c. make cotton into cloth.

10. You can conclude that the demand for cotton today
   - ☐ a. continues to be great.
   - ☐ b. cannot keep up with the supply.
   - ☐ c. is declining.

Correct Answers _____

Written by Hand

All through the early Middle Ages, the only books were those produced by monks. Such books were called manuscripts, which means "written by hand." Before the invention of the printing press, all books were carefully and painstakingly written by hand. The monks who made books were called scribes. All day long, except when they were praying, scribes sat in small rooms copying huge volumes with great patience and skill. In some monasteries, there was a large writing room called a scriptorium. Here all the monks who were skillful writers or illustrators worked together writing books.

There were very strict rules in the scriptorium. No one except the scribes and the head of the monastery were allowed to enter. One monk supervised the work. He had to provide all the necessary materials and give out the work to the others. No one was allowed to speak. Scribes used sign language to make known their needs.

Books in medieval days were not made of paper. Some were written on vellum, which was made from calf's skin. Others were written on parchment made from sheep's skin. The monks prepared the vellum and parchment themselves. Ink was made from soot mixed with gum and acid. Pens were fashioned from goose quills or reeds.

With everything in place, the scribe began the work of writing, slowly forming the large, square, curious-looking Gothic letters in use at that time. Day after day, month after month, the patient scribe bent over his sheets of vellum or parchment, forming each letter perfectly. Over time, the book grew larger and longer. It was often with a sense of relief that a monk finished his long task.

When all the pages were finished, they were usually bound in leather. Some books were covered with velvet, some with delicately carved ivory. Some covers were made of beaten gold and set with pearls and other jewels.

The monks copied Bibles, hymns and prayers, and the lives of saints. They also copied the writings of the Greeks and Romans and other ancient peoples. In this way, they saved the stories and histories that otherwise would have been lost to the world.

The scribes did a great service to civilization. Through their work, many valuable books are preserved for us today. Many of these beautiful books are still kept in museums and libraries, both in Europe and the United States. They are regarded as treasures.

Reading Time _____

Recalling Facts

1. Manuscripts are books
   - ☐ a. written by monks.
   - ☐ b. written by hand.
   - ☐ c. printed on presses.

2. Monks lived in
   - ☐ a. churches.
   - ☐ b. scriptoriums.
   - ☐ c. monasteries.

3. Scribes were monks who
   - ☐ a. made books.
   - ☐ b. built churches.
   - ☐ c. preached.

4. In the early Middle Ages, books were usually bound in
   - ☐ a. paper.
   - ☐ b. fabric.
   - ☐ c. leather.

5. Early pens were made from
   - ☐ a. reeds.
   - ☐ b. gum and acid.
   - ☐ c. leather.

Understanding Ideas

6. You can conclude from the article that books made by monks were mostly
   - ☐ a. works of fiction.
   - ☐ b. original works.
   - ☐ c. copied from other sources.

7. You can conclude from the article that books in medieval times were considered
   - ☐ a. commonplace.
   - ☐ b. rare and valuable.
   - ☐ c. a waste of time.

8. The article suggests that making books
   - ☐ a. was an exciting task.
   - ☐ b. was tedious work.
   - ☐ c. required little skill.

9. It is likely that after the printing press was invented, books
   - ☐ a. continued to be written by hand.
   - ☐ b. became less readable.
   - ☐ c. became more common.

10. The article suggests that without scribes,
   - ☐ a. many early writings would not have been preserved.
   - ☐ b. nothing would be known of early civilizations.
   - ☐ c. there would be no printing presses.

Correct Answers _____

Easier Living with Inventions

The world's progress is due largely to inventions. Whenever a new method, machine, or gadget is invented, it helps people live a little easier, better, or longer. Bit by bit, inventors add to wealth, knowledge, and comfort.

Inventors work with known things and known principles. They combine these in a different way to make a new product or process. A discovery differs from an invention. A discovery is something found in nature that was previously unknown to people. A new chemical substance is an example of a discovery. A new type of engine is an example of an invention.

Today inventions are made in the mechanical, chemical, electronic, and nuclear fields as well as others. New machines and new medicines are developed. New ways of communicating and new uses of energy sources appear often. New inventions lead to new jobs, businesses, and industries. They bring wealth to a nation and help prepare the way for still more inventions.

Invention began with people themselves. Centuries before the invention of writing, people had invented many important new tools. Among these were fire-making devices, the wheel and axle, the pulley, the saw, the screw, the wedge, and the inclined plane. From these simple machines, a great series of inventions have followed. The wheel, for instance, is the basis for all wheeled things, from roller skates to racing cars. It is used also as a water wheel, a potter's wheel, a steering or controlling device, and part of engines—the flywheel, for example.

In days past, many people lived in villages and worked on farms. They baked clay into pottery and wove rushes into baskets. They spun hair, wool, and flax into thread and wove the thread into cloth. They made axes from stone. After a long time, they learned to smelt metals for tools. In time, they invented weights and measures and ways of telling the time and date.

Early people dug wells and irrigation canals. They had drains, sewers, and a water supply around their homes. Gradually, they learned to glaze pottery, work gold and other metals, and make glass for beads. They had lamps for lighting and water clocks for telling time.

Until almost modern times, invention went forward in a hit-or-miss way. There was little science behind it. People progressed only when the need was great and the solution near at hand. Inventions were practical and close to home.

Reading Time _____

Recalling Facts

1. Inventors make new products or processes by
   - ☐ a. working with known things and known principles.
   - ☐ b. making up new principles.
   - ☐ c. finding new things in nature.

2. A discovery is
   - ☐ a. a kind of invention.
   - ☐ b. something found in nature that was formerly unknown.
   - ☐ c. an unnatural process.

3. Roller skates are based on the invention of the
   - ☐ a. wheel.
   - ☐ b. pulley.
   - ☐ c. inclined plane.

4. Among people's earliest inventions were
   - ☐ a. writing implements.
   - ☐ b. clocks.
   - ☐ c. tools.

5. Flax can be
   - ☐ a. smelted for tools.
   - ☐ b. spun into thread.
   - ☐ c. made from stone.

Understanding Ideas

6. Inventions are the result of
   - ☐ a. people's ingenuity.
   - ☐ b. events in nature.
   - ☐ c. natural discoveries.

7. The article suggests that inventions
   - ☐ a. make living conditions worse.
   - ☐ b. improve living conditions.
   - ☐ c. have no effect on living conditions.

8. Compared to earlier inventions, today's inventions are
   - ☐ a. less logical.
   - ☐ b. based on need.
   - ☐ c. more scientific in origin.

9. An example of an invention is
   - ☐ a. a novel made into a film.
   - ☐ b. the computer.
   - ☐ c. a cure for cancer.

10. The next important invention
   - ☐ a. will most likely be in the field of industry.
   - ☐ b. will most likely be atomic in nature.
   - ☐ c. could be in any field.

Correct Answers _____

Lighter Than Air

All of Europe was excited in June 1783. Two brothers, in France, had sent a large paper bag sailing upward into the air. They had filled it with hot smoke from a straw fire. To most people of that day, the soaring bag seemed a miracle. Yet within 50 years, inventors had developed most of the principles used in ballooning today.

Airships were developed from principles of ballooning. Airships, however, have engines with propellers to drive them through the air. They have rudders to steer them. Some airships have a rigid outer fabric. Others are nonrigid and are commonly called blimps. Balloons and airships are classed as lighter-than-air craft. This distinguishes them from airplanes, gliders, and helicopters, which are heavier than air. They have to keep moving and require power from an engine to stay aloft.

A balloon rises because it is filled with a gas that is lighter than air. The total weight of the gas, the balloon bag, and the load it carries must be less than the weight of the air that would occupy the same space (the displaced air). In order to rise, the balloon must be filled with hot air or gases that are lighter than air.

Hydrogen, the lightest gas, catches fire and explodes easily. Coal gas is cheaper, but it is heavier than hydrogen and burns just as easily. Helium, with 93 percent of the lifting power of hydrogen, cannot burn. Although scarce and expensive, it is the ideal balloon gas. The main supply is found in the United States. Its use is government-controlled.

When a toy balloon is blown up by mouth, it falls to the ground. This is because the weight of the rubber and the compressed air in it make it heavier than air. But if it is placed on a radiator so that the air in it becomes hot (not too hot, or it will burst), the balloon expands. It will rise and stay aloft until the air in it cools off. A toy balloon that is filled with helium will float up. It rises until it bursts.

In principle, the round passenger balloon resembles this gas-filled toy. If it is fastened to the ground, it is called a captive balloon. When it is released to drift with the wind, it is a free balloon. The up-and-down motion of a free balloon can be controlled but not its horizontal direction.

Reading Time _____

Recalling Facts

1. Airships were developed from
   - ☐ a. paper bags.
   - ☐ b. ships at sea.
   - ☐ c. principles of ballooning.

2. Airships with nonrigid outer fabric are called
   - ☐ a. balloons.
   - ☐ b. gliders.
   - ☐ c. blimps.

3. Balloons and airships are classed as
   - ☐ a. lighter-than-air craft.
   - ☐ b. heavier-than-air craft.
   - ☐ c. hydrogen craft.

4. The ideal balloon gas is
   - ☐ a. coal.
   - ☐ b. helium.
   - ☐ c. hydrogen.

5. When a toy balloon is blown up by mouth, it
   - ☐ a. rises in the air.
   - ☐ b. falls to the ground.
   - ☐ c. moves horizontally.

Understanding Ideas

6. The fact that helium cannot burn makes it
   - ☐ a. better able to lift balloons.
   - ☐ b. the safest gas for balloons.
   - ☐ c. scarce and expensive.

7. Between airships and balloons,
   - ☐ a. balloons are more dependable as passenger craft.
   - ☐ b. airships are more dependable as passenger craft.
   - ☐ c. both are equally dependable as passenger craft.

8. You can conclude from the article that hot air
   - ☐ a. weighs the same as cool air.
   - ☐ b. is heavier than cool air.
   - ☐ c. is lighter than cool air.

9. Airships and heavier-than-air craft are alike in that both
   - ☐ a. are powered by engines.
   - ☐ b. are fueled by air.
   - ☐ c. float in the air.

10. You can conclude from the article that the up-and-down motion of a free balloon can be controlled by
    - ☐ a. heating the gas within it.
    - ☐ b. a pulley system.
    - ☐ c. releasing the gas within it.

Correct Answers _____

Early Egypt

Ages ago, the land of Egypt was very different from what it is today. Rain fell, and the sea extended far up the Nile Valley. The plateau on each side of the water was grassland. The people wandered over the plateau in search of game and fresh pastures and had no permanent home. They hunted with a crude stone hand ax and with a bow and arrow. Their arrows were made of chipped flint. Very gradually, the rains decreased and the grasslands dried up. The Nile River began to deposit silt in the valley. The animals went down to the valley. The hunters followed them and settled at the edge of the jungle that lined the river.

In the Nile Valley, the people's way of life underwent a great change. They settled down in more or less permanent homes and progressed from food gathering to food producing. They still hunted the elephant and hippopotamus and wild fowl, and they fished in the river. More and more, however, they relied on the animals they bred for meat—long-horned cattle, sheep, goats, and geese.

Early Egyptians learned that the vegetables and wild grain they gathered grew from seeds. When the Nile floodwaters drained away, they dug up the ground with a wooden hoe, scattered seeds over the wet soil, and waited for the harvest. The people raised wheat, barley, a few vegetables, and flax. From the grain they made bread. They spun and wove the flax for linen garments.

The Egyptians' first houses were round or oval, built over a hole in the ground. The walls were lumps of mud, and the roofs were matting. Later houses were rectangular, made of shaped bricks, with wooden frames for doors and windows. The people fashioned ornaments of ivory, made beads and baskets, and carved in stone the figures of people and animals. They built ships that had oars, and they carried on trade with nearby countries.

Good farmland was scarce. The desert came down close to the marshes that edged the river. To gain more land, the people filled in the marshes and built mud walls to keep out the floodwater. In time, they engaged in large-scale irrigation work, digging canals across miles of land. This work required the cooperation of many people living in different places. Leaders became necessary to plan the work and direct the workers. Because of this need, orderly government arose.

Reading Time _____

Recalling Facts

1. Early dwellers of Egypt
   - ☐ a. lived in stone houses.
   - ☐ b. had no permanent homes.
   - ☐ c. lived on the Nile.

2. Early hunters hunted with
   - ☐ a. slingshots.
   - ☐ b. rifles.
   - ☐ c. bows and arrows.

3. The first Egyptian houses were
   - ☐ a. holes in the ground.
   - ☐ b. round or oval.
   - ☐ c. rectangular.

4. Early Egyptian ships were moved by
   - ☐ a. sails.
   - ☐ b. motors.
   - ☐ c. oars.

5. Government arose as a result of
   - ☐ a. the housing industry.
   - ☐ b. a need for planning and organizing work.
   - ☐ c. increased trade.

Understanding Ideas

6. Life changed for early Egyptians mainly because of
   - ☐ a. changes in the climate.
   - ☐ b. flooding of the Nile.
   - ☐ c. enemy invasions.

7. You can conclude from the article that desert land
   - ☐ a. is good for growing certain crops.
   - ☐ b. makes poor farmland.
   - ☐ c. can never be used for farming.

8. You can conclude from the article that farming in Egypt depended on
   - ☐ a. rain.
   - ☐ b. trade with other countries.
   - ☐ c. the Nile.

9. Irrigation is a means of
   - ☐ a. supplying dry land with water.
   - ☐ b. gathering crops.
   - ☐ c. increasing transportation.

10. You can conclude from the article that civilizations are more likely to develop where
   - ☐ a. land is fertile.
   - ☐ b. wild game is plentiful.
   - ☐ c. flooding is frequent.

Correct Answers _____

John Paul Jones

One of the first great American naval heroes was Captain John Paul Jones. A strong, resourceful, and skilled sailor, he loved a battle. His words, "I have not yet begun to fight," are famous throughout the world.

Jones was born on July 6, 1747, in Scotland. When only 12 years old, he was signed on as an apprentice aboard the *Friendship*, a merchant vessel sailing from England to the American colonies.

When the youth finished his apprenticeship, he joined the British navy. Then he became first mate on a slaver, a ship that carried slaves, but soon quit. Ashore in the West Indies, he became an actor. In a single season, he earned enough to sail home as a passenger. On the way, however, the captain and first mate died of typhoid fever. Jones was the only person aboard who could navigate a ship. He guided the ship into port, and the grateful owners kept him on as captain.

At port in the West Indies, Captain Jones had a sailor flogged for mutinous conduct. The sailor left the ship, took berth on another, and died some weeks later. Jones was blamed for the death. He fled his ship. In Virginia and North Carolina, he found old friends. Settling down, he led the placid life of a planter.

When the American Revolution started, he offered his services. His first command was the *Providence*. In 1777, he became captain of the sloop *Ranger*. He carried the news of British General John Bourgoyne's surrender to France. In France, he was given command of the converted merchant ship *Bonhomme Richard*.

On the afternoon of September 23, 1779, the *Bonhomme Richard* engaged the British 44-gun frigate *Serapis* in one of the most famous sea battles in history. For hours, the ships blazed away at each other at short range. Then Jones maneuvered to lash the bowsprit of the *Serapis* to his own ship. The *Bonhomme Richard* was badly damaged, and the English captain called upon Jones to surrender. Jones's proud reply has become a classic retort. "I have not yet begun to fight!" Victory came when an American sailor tossed an exploding grenade into a gunpowder magazine located just below the main deck of the *Serapis*.

After the war, Jones served the new American nation as its agent in Europe. His health was poor and he retired to Paris, where he died on July 18, 1792.

Reading Time _____

Recalling Facts

1. John Paul Jones is considered
   - ☐ a. the first Scottish sea captain.
   - ☐ b. to be one of the first great American naval heroes.
   - ☐ c. a British sea captain during the Revolution.

2. Jones is famous for the words,
   - ☐ a. "If this be treason, make the most of it."
   - ☐ b. "But if they want war, then let it begin here."
   - ☐ c. "I have not yet begun to fight."

3. When only 12 years old, Jones apprenticed aboard a vessel sailing from
   - ☐ a. England to the American colonies.
   - ☐ b. the West Indies to Virginia.
   - ☐ c. the American colonies to France.

4. Jones's first command in the American Revolution was the ship
   - ☐ a. *Friendship.*
   - ☐ b. *Providence.*
   - ☐ c. *Ranger.*

5. The battle between the *Bonhomme Richard* and the *Serapis* was
   - ☐ a. a sea battle between France and Great Britain.
   - ☐ b. the last sea battle of the Revolutionary War.
   - ☐ c. one of the most famous sea battles in history.

Understanding Ideas

6. A word that describes John Paul Jones as a youth is
   - ☐ a. loyal.
   - ☐ b. studious.
   - ☐ c. adventurous.

7. Jones became a ship's captain due to
   - ☐ a. hard work.
   - ☐ b. luck.
   - ☐ c. wealth.

8. By offering his services to the American war effort, Jones showed his
   - ☐ a. cowardice.
   - ☐ b. patriotism.
   - ☐ c. stubbornness.

9. Jones's appointment as America's agent in Europe shows that he was
   - ☐ a. admired by his peers.
   - ☐ b. highly educated.
   - ☐ c. tired of fighting.

10. Jones's words during the battle with the *Serapis* suggest that he was
   - ☐ a. close to victory.
   - ☐ b. likely to surrender.
   - ☐ c. too proud to surrender.

Correct Answers _____

Problem Drinking

13

An overwhelming desire to drink alcohol is a disease called alcoholism. Alcohol is a drug; it causes harm. In the United States, alcoholism is the most widespread form of drug abuse. Alcoholism affects at least five million persons. About one-third of high school students in the United States are thought to be problem drinkers. Many may be alcoholics. Drunk drivers account for one-half of all fatal automobile accidents each year. Drinking is a leading cause of loss of income. Heavy drinkers display social and personal problems.

Alcoholism also creates many severe physical problems. More than three drinks a day over even a few weeks causes destructive changes in the liver. About 15 percent of heavy drinkers develop cirrhosis, a liver disease that can be fatal. Changes in the brain and nervous system result in hostile behavior, loss of mental sharpness, and poor judgment. One-third of the babies born to mothers who drink heavily have birth defects or retardation. This condition is called fetal alcohol syndrome. Some drugs, such as tranquilizers, when taken with alcohol can result in death.

It has long been thought that alcohol abuse resulted from a combination of psychological and social factors. Current scientific research suggests that a tendency to abuse alcohol runs in families. An inherited chemical defect could play a role. Researchers have discovered a rare gene, possibly one of several that may lead to alcoholism. This suggests that in some cases the disease may be inherited.

A family or individual with an alcohol problem is in serious trouble. The alcoholic's main goal is to get something to drink. The drinking usually continues until the victim is drunk. Family, work, and friends are of little concern when there is a need for alcohol. Drunkenness inhibits the alcoholic's control of normal behavior. It depresses the ability to perform even the simplest functions.

Alcoholics can be helped. Two absolute rules apply to their recovery. An alcoholic must accept the fact that there is a real problem and decide to stop drinking. Second, the patient must also realize that any form or quantity of alcohol is literally poison. Most treatment experts believe that an alcoholic can never take another drink. Alcoholism is a lifelong condition.

Since the late 1940s, Antabuse and other drugs have been used to prevent drinking. The drug causes a violent physical reaction when alcohol is consumed. Problem drinkers can and are being helped.

Reading Time _____

Recalling Facts

1. In the United States, alcoholism affects
   - [ ] a. adults only.
   - [ ] b. at least five million persons.
   - [ ] c. most people.

2. One-half of all fatal automobile accidents each year are caused by
   - [ ] a. teenagers.
   - [ ] b. bad weather.
   - [ ] c. drunk drivers.

3. Scientific research suggests that alcohol abuse
   - [ ] a. runs in families.
   - [ ] b. is most frequent in rural areas.
   - [ ] c. leads to drug addiction.

4. Antabuse helps prevent drinking by
   - [ ] a. eliminating the desire to drink.
   - [ ] b. causing a violent physical reaction when alcohol is consumed.
   - [ ] c. inhibiting the alcoholic's mental function.

5. Alcohol abuse causes cirrhosis, or damage to the
   - [ ] a. nervous system.
   - [ ] b. brain.
   - [ ] c. liver.

Understanding Ideas

6. The article suggests that recovery from alcoholism depends mainly on
   - [ ] a. whether the disease is inherited.
   - [ ] b. the alcoholic's decision to stop drinking.
   - [ ] c. resources available to the alcoholic.

7. You can conclude from the article that alcoholics
   - [ ] a. can limit their drinking.
   - [ ] b. suffer no physical harm from drinking.
   - [ ] c. can cause problems for families and friends.

8. You can conclude from the article that the effects of alcoholism
   - [ ] a. are primarily physical.
   - [ ] b. include physical, economic, and social problems.
   - [ ] c. are not very important.

9. Alcoholism is the most widespread form of drug abuse in the United States, which suggests that
   - [ ] a. most Americans are problem drinkers.
   - [ ] b. Americans need better education about the harmful effects of alcohol.
   - [ ] c. people in the United States should not be allowed to drink alcohol.

10. You can conclude from the article that causes of alcoholism are
    - [ ] a. well understood.
    - [ ] b. still being researched.
    - [ ] c. usually psychological.

Correct Answers _____

Rabbits and Hares

Cottontails and jackrabbits are among the best-known wild animals. They are abundant in the brushy woods and gardens of eastern North America, on the western plains and deserts, on mountains, and even in the Arctic snows.

Many of the animals called rabbits are actually hares. The hare is larger and heavier and has longer ears. With its longer hind legs and larger hind feet, it can outjump any rabbit and does not tire as quickly. Many hares turn white in the winter. Rabbits keep the same color coat year-round.

Hares and rabbits bear their young in very different ways. The female hare (called a doe) has two or three litters of young a year, with four to six babies in each litter. She does not make a nest. The young are born in a flattened area called a form, in the grass beneath a low branch, or under a brush heap. Young jackrabbits, which are hares, may lie directly on the desert ground in the shade of a cactus or other plant. Young hares are born with their eyes open and with thick fur on their bodies. They can care for themselves within a few days.

A mother rabbit provides a nest by scraping out a hollow in the grass or moving into an old woodchuck hole. The young are born blind, without fur, and helpless. The mother feeds the babies with her milk. When she goes for her own food, she hides the nest with leaves or grass. The baby rabbits open their eyes in about a week. After birth, they leave the nest to explore within 10 to 12 days. By the time they are three weeks old, they can care for themselves. Rabbits have many litters from early spring to late fall. There are four to six young in each litter. In the southern states, rabbits bear young throughout the year. Male rabbits and hares (called bucks) pay no attention to the young.

Rabbits and hares are gnawing animals like rats, mice, and squirrels. They have the same type of strong, chisel-like front teeth.

Rabbits and hares feed at night and remain in the nest or form during the day. They are fond of all green growing things and have thus earned the reputation of doing great damage to gardens and field crops. In the winter, they feed on the bark of trees and shrubs, on buds, and on berries.

Reading Time _____

Recalling Facts

1. Compared to rabbits, hares are
   - ☐ a. smaller and less quick.
   - ☐ b. larger and heavier.
   - ☐ c. short-eared.

2. The female hare is called a
   - ☐ a. jackrabbit.
   - ☐ b. doe.
   - ☐ c. nurse.

3. Young hares become independent
   - ☐ a. within a few days.
   - ☐ b. within a year.
   - ☐ c. after a year.

4. In a year, rabbits have
   - ☐ a. one litter.
   - ☐ b. two litters.
   - ☐ c. many litters.

5. Male rabbits are known for
   - ☐ a. protecting their young.
   - ☐ b. ignoring their young.
   - ☐ c. eating their young.

Understanding Ideas

6. Compared to young rabbits, young hares
   - ☐ a. are independent sooner.
   - ☐ b. are dependent longer.
   - ☐ c. leave the nest at the same time.

7. It is likely that the dense fur on the bodies of young hares
   - ☐ a. constantly changes color.
   - ☐ b. falls out as they age.
   - ☐ c. helps to protect them.

8. You can conclude from the article that a mother rabbit
   - ☐ a. must be very protective of her young.
   - ☐ b. pays little attention to her young.
   - ☐ c. pushes her young out of the nest.

9. It is likely that rabbits and hares feed at night because
   - ☐ a. it is cooler.
   - ☐ b. it is easier to conceal themselves from enemies.
   - ☐ c. food is more plentiful then.

10. You can conclude that rabbits and hares
    - ☐ a. are becoming scarce.
    - ☐ b. live only in warmer climates.
    - ☐ c. are very adaptable creatures.

Correct Answers _____

Save the Watershed

A watershed is the area drained by a river or a stream. Such an area slopes toward a common land trough. Some rain runs off, or drains, over the the ground surface. Runoff water forms small streams, which flow into larger ones. These in time join to form rivers.

A natural watershed conserves water. It has clear streams and a cover of trees, grasses, and other plants. Plants help form a part of the topsoil called humus. Humus consists of rotting leaves and wood, bacteria, fungi, dead insects, and other plant and animal remains. It provides some of the nutrients for new plant life. Along with a network of roots, humus acts as a blotter that soaks up rain. Plants break the force of falling rain and scatter the drops over leaves and branches. Some of the water returns to the air by evaporation. Some of the water used by plants is passed through their leaves into the air again by transpiration. The rest of the water sinks into the earth through countless tiny channels. Some of the spaces through which water drains are caused by natural features of the land or soil itself. Others are made by plant roots and burrowing animals like earthworms, insects, and moles.

The level at which the earth has always been saturated is known as the water table. This vast water supply under the ground changes with the seasons and the amount of rainfall. During long, heavy rains, the soil may not be able to soak up all the water. Some of it runs off the surface. In a forest watershed, it moves slowly. Deep snow that melts slowly allows water to soak into the soil gradually.

Sometimes trees in an area have been cut down due to poor forestry practices. Grasses and other plants may have been stripped off by fire, overgrazing, or poor farming practices. The water from rainfall then flows over the ground instead of being absorbed by the plant growth that once was there.

Mud closes the channels through which water sinks into the soil. If the land is level, the water stands in stagnant pools. If it slopes, the water runs downhill into the rivers. Streams become brown with silt because the racing water carries soil along with it. In the spring, heavy rains and melting snows overflow the riverbanks. In the summer, streams, springs, and wells can dry up.

Reading Time _____

Recalling Facts

1. A watershed is
   - ☐ a. a river or stream.
   - ☐ b. the area at the mouth of a river.
   - ☐ c. the area drained by a river or a stream.

2. A natural watershed
   - ☐ a. creates a waterfall.
   - ☐ b. conserves water.
   - ☐ c. provides the power for electricity.

3. The level at which the earth has always been saturated is known as
   - ☐ a. the water table.
   - ☐ b. humus.
   - ☐ c. a natural watershed.

4. The underground supply of water changes with the seasons and
   - ☐ a. water conservation.
   - ☐ b. the amount of rainfall.
   - ☐ c. the tilt of the earth.

5. If land slopes, water
   - ☐ a. runs downhill into rivers.
   - ☐ b. becomes stagnant.
   - ☐ c. evaporates more quickly.

Understanding Ideas

6. Water moves slowly over the surface of a forest watershed because
   - ☐ a. there are no plants to absorb the water.
   - ☐ b. plant growth absorbs the water gradually.
   - ☐ c. fences stem the flow.

7. Watersheds are important to
   - ☐ a. wildlife preservation.
   - ☐ b. industrial pollution.
   - ☐ c. water conservation.

8. You can conclude from the article that silt
   - ☐ a. is a part of the soil.
   - ☐ b. is dangerous to plants and animals.
   - ☐ c. causes water to stagnate.

9. It is likely that without watersheds,
   - ☐ a. there would be no drinkable water.
   - ☐ b. rivers and streams would dry up.
   - ☐ c. the water supply would decrease.

10. For their water supply, watersheds depend on
    - ☐ a. rain and snow.
    - ☐ b. rivers and streams.
    - ☐ c. humus.

Correct Answers _____

The Acropolis

16

More than 2,300 years ago, the Greeks used white marble to create the most beautiful temples and statues in the ancient world. The best of these stood upon the Acropolis, a plateau in the heart of Athens. An oblong mass of rock, the Acropolis looks very much like a pedestal. Its almost flat top covers slightly less than eight acres (3.3 hectares).

Perhaps 4,000 years ago, the earliest people of Athens walled in the Acropolis for protection. Here their first kings ruled and in later years, Acropolis held the chief shrines of Athena, Greek goddess of war and wisdom. More than 2,500 years ago, the shrines began to rise. Only 90 years later, the Spartans found the Acropolis covered with marble temples and dwellings. They destroyed the dwellings, but they paused in awe and silence before the temples and left them unharmed.

In 480 BC, the Persians burned or smashed everything on the Acropolis. In 447 BC, the sculptor Phidias was placed in charge of restoring the Acropolis. Several years before, he had erected a large bronze statue of Athena on the Acropolis. Now he began to build her a shrine. This Doric temple, called the Parthenon (dwelling of the maiden), was opened in 438 BC.

On the western side of the Parthenon stood statues of Athena and Poseidon, the sea god. Relief carvings studded the outside. Along the portico, between the temple's outside columns and its walls, was a frieze. It extended around the top of the walls. Its images represented the procession that carried a new gown to Athena each year. In the temple was another statue of Athena. Its body was made of ivory and its dress of gold. Its right hand held a statue of Nike, goddess of victory, and its left hand rested upon a shield. A majestic gate was erected at the west end of the Acropolis.

By the 5th century AD, the Byzantines had made the Parthenon a Christian church. Ten centuries later, the Turks made it a mosque. In 1687, under attack by the Venetians, the Turks stored gunpowder in the mosque. Struck by a cannonball, it exploded, killing 300 people. The roof, walls, and 16 columns lay in ruin.

In 1829, Greece began to redeem the ruins. Some fallen pillars have been restored in the Parthenon, but it is still empty and roofless. It suffered further damage in World War II.

Reading Time _____

Recalling Facts

1. The Acropolis is a
   - ☐ a. white marble statue.
   - ☐ b. small, rocky plateau.
   - ☐ c. Greek temple.

2. The first kings of Athens ruled about
   - ☐ a. 2,000 years ago.
   - ☐ b. 4,000 years ago.
   - ☐ c. 6,000 years ago.

3. The Parthenon was built as a
   - ☐ a. Christian church.
   - ☐ b. palace for a king.
   - ☐ c. shrine to Athena.

4. The Parthenon was destroyed by
   - ☐ a. a cannonball.
   - ☐ b. the Spartans.
   - ☐ c. the effects of time.

5. The Greeks worshipped Nike, goddess of
   - ☐ a. sport.
   - ☐ b. victory.
   - ☐ c. love.

Understanding Ideas

6. You can conclude from the article that Athens was named for the
   - ☐ a. sea god.
   - ☐ b. goddess of victory.
   - ☐ c. goddess of wisdom.

7. It is likely that the Parthenon is still in ruins because
   - ☐ a. Greeks prefer ruins to restored buildings.
   - ☐ b. it cannot be restored.
   - ☐ c. the cost of restoration is great.

8. You can conclude that ancient Greeks
   - ☐ a. cared little for religion.
   - ☐ b. were quite religious.
   - ☐ c. were Christians.

9. The fact that the Greeks used white marble for their temples and statues suggests that
   - ☐ a. white was considered a holy color.
   - ☐ b. no other stone existed.
   - ☐ c. marble was readily available.

10. You can conclude that by the 15th century AD, Athens
    - ☐ a. was under Greek rule.
    - ☐ b. was controlled by the Turks.
    - ☐ c. had been totally destroyed.

Correct Answers _____

The Cowpuncher's Partner

17

In the culture of the western plains, cowhands, or cowpunchers, as they preferred to call themselves, stood out as some of the most important figures. The people, the clothes they wore, and the horses they rode were all outgrowths of life on the range. The job of driving, roping, and handling cattle required expert riding skills.

The most important possession of all cowpunchers, their partner in every detail of their work, was their horse. It was a tough wiry animal called a bronco. It may have descended from the horses brought into the Southwest by the Spaniards. The bronco was born on the range and ran wild until it was two or three years old. Then the horse was rounded up and driven into the ranch corral. There, its training as a cow horse began.

The horse was first taught to never "run on a rope." Then it learned how to lead. That means to follow at the pull of a rope or rein, instead of holding back. Next, the bronco was saddled and allowed to wear itself out in the hopeless effort to throw off the saddle.

After a few days of such schooling, a bitless bridle was slipped on the horse's head. A blindfold was passed over its eyes, and the broncobuster got into the saddle. As soon as the blindfold was removed, the bronco would usually rear and try to throw its rider.

To hold that job, broncobusters had to stay with the majority of their mounts on this first ride. A horse that started out with the impression that it was easy to throw a person might turn into an outlaw, making the horse useless for serious work. When the half-broken horse learned to take a bit without hurting its mouth, it was turned over to the cowpunchers. They taught the bronco the finishing touches that would make it a good cow horse.

The cowpuncher's saddle was heavy. It sometimes weighed 40 pounds (18 kilograms) or more. A broad cinch, or girth of woven cord, went under the horse's belly. Sometimes, especially when heavy roping had to be done, a second cinch was used. In front of the wide, deep saddle seat was a horn. The rider sat straight-legged, feet flat in the stirrups. Sometimes these stirrups were protected by heavy leather hoods.

Reading Time _____

Recalling Facts

1. Early cowhands preferred to call themselves
   - ☐ a. riders.
   - ☐ b. cowpunchers.
   - ☐ c. cowpokes.

2. Cowpunchers' valued partner was their
   - ☐ a. saddle.
   - ☐ b. rope.
   - ☐ c. bronco.

3. Broncos were trained
   - ☐ a. right after birth.
   - ☐ b. when they were two or three years old.
   - ☐ c. after being blindfolded.

4. In front of a cowpuncher's saddle sat a
   - ☐ a. pie.
   - ☐ b. horn.
   - ☐ c. box.

5. The part of the saddle holding a rider's feet is called
   - ☐ a. stirrups.
   - ☐ b. cinches.
   - ☐ c. reins.

Understanding Ideas

6. A good broncobuster would have to be
   - ☐ a. an excellent rider.
   - ☐ b. a cowhand.
   - ☐ c. light in weight.

7. Broncos were trained mainly
   - ☐ a. to compete in rodeos.
   - ☐ b. for work.
   - ☐ c. as a means of transportation.

8. Broncos were used as cow horses probably because
   - ☐ a. they had to be trained.
   - ☐ b. they were easy to round up.
   - ☐ c. they were tough and wiry.

9. A half-broken horse was one that
   - ☐ a. had a broken leg.
   - ☐ b. was partially trained.
   - ☐ c. would become an outlaw.

10. You can conclude from the article that cattle raising was
    - ☐ a. important to the livelihood of early westerners.
    - ☐ b. mainly an eastern tradition.
    - ☐ c. rare in the early West.

Correct Answers _____

Try Jogging for Fitness

18

Running for fitness, exercise, and pleasure is commonly called jogging. It has become very popular in recent years. The popularity of jogging today stems from several factors. First, jogging is one of the most efficient forms of exercise. As a rule, a person jogging burns up more calories per minute than in most other sports. Running, like biking, swimming, and brisk walking, is an aerobic exercise. Such an exercise uses a great deal of oxygen. In addition, it increases the heart rate. Aerobic exercise strengthens the heart muscle so that it pumps more efficiently. This kind of exercise is also one of the best ways to improve the general health and capacity of the lungs.

Jogging is also popular because almost everyone can take part. Jogging is an activity that doesn't require any unusual skills or special coordination. Jogging is relaxing and fun. Finally, it can be done alone, with another person, or in a group.

The same number of calories (about 100 for most men and 80 for most women) is burned walking a mile as running a mile. Thus, one of the best ways to begin a jogging program is to combine it with a walking program. Increases in the amount of jogging should come gradually. The jogger who experiences dizziness, tightness of the chest, or nausea should slow down. If the discomfort is great, the jogger should consult a doctor before running again.

For anyone who runs more than 10 miles (16 kilometers) a week, it is important to have good running shoes. Tennis shoes or sneakers won't do. Running produces stress that is three times greater than the stress of walking. With this added stress to the feet and legs, a jogger needs good shoes. The shoes should be replaced when they are worn out or worn unevenly.

Cold weather poses few problems for joggers. The main hazard in winter running is slipping on ice or snow. There is no danger of freezing the lungs, because the body warms the air before it reaches the lungs. Winter joggers should be sure to cover the head and extremities and keep their feet as dry and warm as possible. It is best to wear layers of clothing.

In summer, joggers must be careful not to dry out. Drinking plenty of water on hot, humid days is important. The best summer wear is loose fitting and light colored.

Reading Time _____

Recalling Facts

1. Aerobic exercise increases
   - ☐ a. the size of the heart.
   - ☐ b. the heart rate.
   - ☐ c. chest tightness.

2. Briskly walking a mile burns about
   - ☐ a. eight to 10 calories.
   - ☐ b. 80 to 100 calories.
   - ☐ c. 800 to 1,000 calories.

3. Jogging is a popular form of exercise in part because it
   - ☐ a. takes very little time.
   - ☐ b. is an inefficient form of exercise.
   - ☐ c. requires no special skills.

4. The stress of running is
   - ☐ a. three times greater than the stress of walking.
   - ☐ b. three times less than the stress of walking.
   - ☐ c. about the same as the stress of walking.

5. The main hazard of winter running is
   - ☐ a. freezing the lungs.
   - ☐ b. cold, wet feet.
   - ☐ c. slipping on ice or snow.

Understanding Ideas

6. One of the best ways to stay in shape is by
   - ☐ a. burning up calories.
   - ☐ b. exercising aerobically.
   - ☐ c. working out for long periods of time.

7. It is likely that people like jogging because
   - ☐ a. it causes heavy breathing.
   - ☐ b. doctors recommend it.
   - ☐ c. it is an easy way to stay in shape.

8. To get the most from the exercise, joggers should
   - ☐ a. increase their heart rate.
   - ☐ b. train for several weeks.
   - ☐ c. run as fast as they can.

9. Good running shoes are important because
   - ☐ a. joggers can run faster.
   - ☐ b. they keep the feet warm and dry.
   - ☐ c. they help absorb the stress of jogging.

10. You can conclude from the article that jogging is popular
   - ☐ a. mostly in warm-weather areas.
   - ☐ b. in a variety of climates.
   - ☐ c. mostly in cold-weather areas.

Correct Answers _____

Unit 1

Reading Rate

Instructions: Put an X on the line above each lesson number to show your reading time and words-per-minute rate for that lesson.

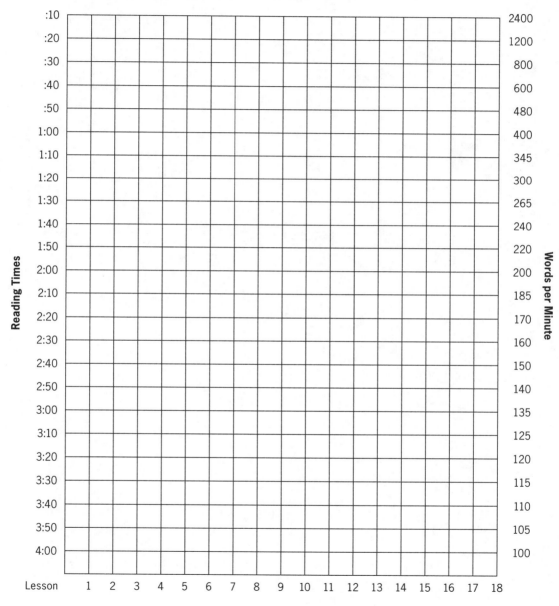

Unit 1

Comprehension Score

Instructions: Put an X on the line above each lesson number to indicate your total correct answers and comprehension score for that lesson.

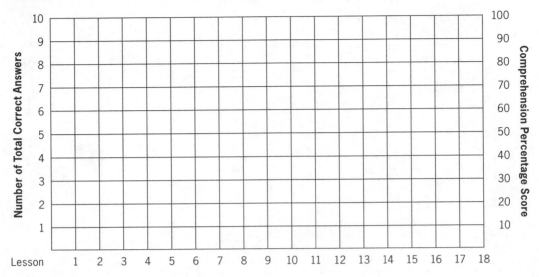

The Birthplace of Human Beings

People can only guess where human beings first appeared on the earth. In this case, *guessing* means drawing a conclusion from all the facts that can be found. The conclusion may fit the known facts, but it cannot be proved by the actual evidence. A commonly accepted conclusion is that Asia is the birthplace of humans.

There are facts that support this conclusion. People may have developed from an apelike ancestor common to humans and other primates. The lands where animals have developed over thousands of years have had mild climates, various kinds of landscapes, and enough, but not too much, food.

At a point in time, a few million years before humans appeared, there was a vast plateau in northern Asia. The climate there was neither cold nor tropical. When not in search of food, animals were not always resting. They roved around looking for new sources of food. On this plateau, there were forests, plains, and open land. Some of these places had plenty of rain. Others were deserts. Many of the plants were good to eat, and there was plenty of game.

The very earliest humans probably dwelled on the floor of the forests. There, they could use the trees as shelters. Those who ventured onto the plains had to be alert to avoid the floods and sandstorms that caught and preserved so many animals. The ability to escape provided for future generations, but left no evidence of the past.

There were primates in Asia before the earliest records of humans. The primates were different from the primates and humans of today, but they could have been the ancestors of either or both.

Some of the first human-like creatures were found in Asia, and many possible ancestors of humans were also found there. Asia seems a probable homeland for humanity.

However, there is room for disagreement. No one disputes that humans could have developed in Asia. But researchers point out that the same conditions on other continents could have led to the same development. Africa is one example. Conditions there were much the same in ancient times. Moreover, the most humanlike apes live there today.

People will have to wait for the discovery of more fossil bones and the study of them before they can know positively which continent was the birthplace of humans.

Reading Time _____

Recalling Facts

1. A likely place for humans' first appearance is
   - ☐ a. South America.
   - ☐ b. Asia.
   - ☐ c. Australia.

2. It is possible that humans descended from
   - ☐ a. early plants.
   - ☐ b. fossils.
   - ☐ c. primates.

3. One argument that favors Africa as the birthplace of humans states that
   - ☐ a. the most human-like apes today live there.
   - ☐ b. more fossil bones are found there.
   - ☐ c. much of Africa is desert.

4. The first humans probably
   - ☐ a. lived on the floor of the forest.
   - ☐ b. were desert dwellers.
   - ☐ c. were tree dwellers.

5. Conclusions about human beings' birthplace are based on
   - ☐ a. imaginative guesses.
   - ☐ b. available facts.
   - ☐ c. the discovery of ancient writings.

Understanding Ideas

6. The earliest humans probably fared best in
   - ☐ a. tropical climates.
   - ☐ b. cold climates.
   - ☐ c. mild climates.

7. You can conclude from the article that scientists
   - ☐ a. have determined the location of humans' birthplace.
   - ☐ b. will continue to investigate humans' birthplace.
   - ☐ c. have determined little about humans' birthplace.

8. You can conclude that the determination of humans' birthplace depends largely on
   - ☐ a. new discoveries.
   - ☐ b. guesswork.
   - ☐ c. reexamining known facts.

9. You can conclude that the environment of present-day Africa
   - ☐ a. is different from that of northern Asia in the past.
   - ☐ b. cannot be compared to that of northern Asia in the past.
   - ☐ c. is similar to that of northern Asia in the past.

10. The article suggests that the final determination of humans' birthplace
    - ☐ a. will probably never be made.
    - ☐ b. is likely to be made someday.
    - ☐ c. should remain a mystery.

Correct Answers _____

FUSION Reading *Plus*

Thomas Jefferson

20

Thomas Jefferson was the third president of the United States. He was also the author of the Declaration of Independence and the Virginia Statute for Religious Freedom. In an age of greatness, Jefferson was noted for his curious mind. He was a farmer, scientist, architect, and inventor as well as a government leader. He helped the United States get started, and his plans for the future helped it grow. Many of the good things Americans enjoy today have come from Jefferson's devotion to human rights.

Jefferson was a tall, straight-bodied, well-proportioned person. He stood and walked straight and his shoulders were always square. He had hazel eyes and a long, high nose. His hair was reddish, becoming sandy as he grew older. Unlike other gentlemen of his day, he never wore a wig.

In the fashion of his time, Jefferson dressed in a long, dark coat; a ruffled cravat (in place of the modern necktie); a red waistcoat, short knee breeches; and shoes with big, bright buckles. Except in his days of courtship and married life, he paid little attention to clothes. When he was president of the United States, Jefferson made a habit of plainness, both in his personal appearance and in matters of ceremony.

Jefferson was a courteous person, bowing to everyone he met. People found him to be mild and pleasant. He was reserved, and no one ever called him by his first name. He was a very poor public speaker in a day of great orators. He talked in a thin, fine voice.

He loved music, played the violin well, liked to sing, and usually hummed or sang as he walked or rode. A good horseback rider, he often rode for pleasure when people generally rode only as a means of travel.

About 37 years after Jefferson's death, Abraham Lincoln described the American government as "of the people, by the people, for the people." He was defining the kind of government that Jefferson, more than any other official, had made possible. Even Jefferson's closest coworkers thought of human rights as including the protection of life and liberty and, above all, of private property.

"Give the people light," said Jefferson, "and they will find their own way." He meant all the people.

Reading Time _____

Recalling Facts

1. Thomas Jefferson was the United States'
   - ☐ a. first president.
   - ☐ b. second president.
   - ☐ c. third president.

2. Thomas Jefferson was not an author of the
   - ☐ a. Declaration of Independence.
   - ☐ b. Constitution of the United States.
   - ☐ c. Virginia Statute for Religious Freedom.

3. Jefferson was known
   - ☐ a. as a fine orator.
   - ☐ b. for his devotion to human rights.
   - ☐ c. as an open, friendly person.

4. Jefferson could play
   - ☐ a. a variety of musical instruments.
   - ☐ b. the guitar.
   - ☐ c. the violin well.

5. Most gentlemen of Jefferson's time
   - ☐ a. cared little about their appearance.
   - ☐ b. did not wear wigs.
   - ☐ c. wore red vests and bright shoe buckles.

Understanding Ideas

6. The characteristic that most qualified Thomas Jefferson for the presidency was probably his
   - ☐ a. curious mind.
   - ☐ b. horse riding ability.
   - ☐ c. plainness.

7. You can conclude from the article that the Declaration of Independence guaranteed Americans
   - ☐ a. human rights.
   - ☐ b. wealth.
   - ☐ c. a strong government.

8. You can conclude that Thomas Jefferson was a talented
   - ☐ a. singer.
   - ☐ b. writer.
   - ☐ c. public speaker.

9. If Thomas Jefferson were alive today, he would most likely support
   - ☐ a. educational scholarships.
   - ☐ b. the fashion industry.
   - ☐ c. a dictator.

10. You can conclude that Jefferson's ideas about government
    - ☐ a. agreed with those of his coworkers.
    - ☐ b. would be unacceptable today.
    - ☐ c. were ahead of his time.

Correct Answers _____

Early Weapons and Defenses

21

For many centuries, the sword was the chief weapon of war. Defenses against it were gradually invented. The best defense was another sword. Next, a stout shield was found to be a great help. Early shields were made of heavy leather over a wood framework. Later came metal shields. A defender used the shield to parry the blow of an opponent's sword while driving home his own weapon. The shield eventually grew larger and longer. A warrior could hide almost completely behind it. But this type of shield proved too heavy and unwieldy. With it, a battler could move only slowly and with great difficulty.

To use a three-foot (1-meter) sword effectively, a fighter had to be within three feet of the enemy. At such short distances, however, the fighter was in turn easily within reach of the opponent's sword. Being able to fight at greater distances would protect the fighters. They gained this distance by using spears, javelins, lances, and similar weapons with sharp points on long shafts. Spears were lightweight and well balanced so that they could be thrown with great accuracy.

Longer and heavier spears were used for thrusting rather than throwing. They were especially deadly when held firmly in the grip of a horse rider moving at full tilt. With the horse, warriors gained the advantage of speed and movement in battle.

During the Middle Ages, armed and armored knights on horseback became the heroic figures of warfare. The spears they used were so long and heavy that the knights rested them on saddle braces. At this time, playing war games became more popular than war itself. Great jousting tournaments were held at the principal courts of Europe. At these celebrated events, special jousting spears were used. They were blunt-ended, and the opponents were well covered with armor so that little blood was spilled.

Suits of armor were cleverly made so that overlapping steel plates allowed the bending of joints and easier movement than one might suspect. Even horses were armored. A knight in heavy armor was at great risk, however, when thrown from a horse. On the ground, the knight could easily be surrounded by serfs armed with pikes. Pikes were spears up to 24 feet (7 meters) in length. They were carried by the lowly infantry, which made up most of the fighting force. Only the rich and lordly rode out to battle in shining armor.

Reading Time _____

Recalling Facts

1. The best defense against a sword was
   - ☐ a. another sword.
   - ☐ b. a spear.
   - ☐ c. a stout shield.

2. The earliest shields were made of
   - ☐ a. strong cloth on wood.
   - ☐ b. metal.
   - ☐ c. heavy leather.

3. Spears used for thrusting rather than throwing were
   - ☐ a. shorter and heavier.
   - ☐ b. shorter and lighter.
   - ☐ c. longer and heavier.

4. During the Middle Ages, the heroic figures in warfare were the
   - ☐ a. knights.
   - ☐ b. infantry soldiers.
   - ☐ c. serfs.

5. The infantry was composed of
   - ☐ a. knights.
   - ☐ b. lords.
   - ☐ c. serfs.

Understanding Ideas

6. You can conclude from the article that the best weapon for close combat was a
   - ☐ a. jousting spear.
   - ☐ b. sword.
   - ☐ c. javelin.

7. A soldier in armor and on horseback was probably
   - ☐ a. from the lower classes.
   - ☐ b. a member of the upper classes.
   - ☐ c. in the infantry.

8. You can conclude that armor and a shield
   - ☐ a. prevented bloodshed.
   - ☐ b. were useful only for horseback riders.
   - ☐ c. helped prevent bloodshed.

9. You can conclude that very large metal shields
   - ☐ a. had both advantages and disadvantages.
   - ☐ b. were less troublesome than harmful.
   - ☐ c. were best suited for poor fighters.

10. The article suggests that during the Middle Ages, war was considered
    - ☐ a. shameful.
    - ☐ b. amusing.
    - ☐ c. extravagant.

Correct Answers _____

He Wrote *Robinson Crusoe*

The author of *Robinson Crusoe* was Daniel Defoe. A man of many talents, he was not only a writer, but also a business person, secret agent, and journalist.

Daniel Defoe was born in London, England, in about 1660. His father, James Foe, was a butcher and a candle maker. The Foes were Dissenters who did not believe in certain practices of the Church of England. Daniel was brought up in the strict, yet independent beliefs of the Dissenters.

At 14, Daniel was sent to a Dissenters' academy. In addition to traditional Latin and Greek, he studied French, Italian, Spanish, and history. He became especially well educated in geography. Although he studied for the ministry, Daniel went into business.

Engaged in foreign trade, Daniel visited France and lived in Spain for a time. Meanwhile, he was writing and speculating financially. He began to use the name Defoe, which may have been the original Flemish family name.

Defoe soon became more interested in writing than in conducting business. He was concerned about the many problems of the day. In pamphlets, verse, and periodicals, he called for reforms and advances in religious practices, economics, social welfare, and politics. In 1698, he wrote "Essay on Projects." In it, Defoe suggested a national bank, reformed bankruptcy laws, asylums, and academies of learning. He stressed the need for tolerance, often using satire for emphasis.

In 1702, Defoe wrote a pamphlet satirizing the persecution of Dissenters titled "The Shortest Way with the Dissenters." The government arrested him; for three days, he stood locked in irons while people brought him flowers. They admired his spirit. Defoe wrote of this experience.

After some months in prison, Defoe was released through the influence of Robert Harley, a politician who became his patron. Defoe then wrote political pamphlets for Harley and served as his secret agent working for the union of Scotland and England.

In 1704, Defoe started *The Review*, which was the first of many such periodicals with which he was connected. As people of that era did not care for fiction, Defoe wrote histories of pirates and thieves, spicing facts with imagination. In 1719, he published the novel *Robinson Crusoe*, which was drawn from the experiences of British sailor Alexander Selkirk. Like the character in the novel, Selkirk was marooned on a Pacific island for several years.

Defoe's other major works include *Moll Flanders* and *Roxana*. He died in London on April 24, 1731.

Reading Time _____

Recalling Facts

1. Daniel Defoe was born in
   - ☐ a. Spain.
   - ☐ b. France.
   - ☐ c. England.

2. Dissenters were people who
   - ☐ a. disagreed with some practices of the Church of England.
   - ☐ b. agreed with the practices of the Church of England.
   - ☐ c. did not follow any organized religion.

3. Defoe went into business after studying to be a
   - ☐ a. lawyer.
   - ☐ b. teacher.
   - ☐ c. minister.

4. After writing a satire about the persecution of the Dissenters, Defoe
   - ☐ a. was imprisoned.
   - ☐ b. changed his name to Defoe.
   - ☐ c. moved to Scotland.

5. *Robinson Crusoe* was based on
   - ☐ a. Defoe's own travels.
   - ☐ b. the experiences of Alexander Selkirk, a British sailor.
   - ☐ c. Robert Harley's adventures.

Understanding Ideas

6. Defoe's earliest works suggest that he might have been a good
   - ☐ a. doctor.
   - ☐ b. judge.
   - ☐ c. politician.

7. Defoe's use of satire exhibited his
   - ☐ a. serious nature.
   - ☐ b. acting ability.
   - ☐ c. sense of humor.

8. Defoe received flowers while in jail, which suggests that
   - ☐ a. he was wrongly imprisoned.
   - ☐ b. the government misestimated the popularity of his ideas.
   - ☐ c. all prisoners received flowers.

9. A good word to describe Daniel Defoe is
   - ☐ a. defiant.
   - ☐ b. timid.
   - ☐ c. indifferent.

10. Defoe would probably support the need for
    - ☐ a. greater understanding of differences among people and ideas.
    - ☐ b. state religions.
    - ☐ c. censorship of ideas.

Correct Answers _____

The Earliest Writing

23

Very early on, people must have felt the need to send messages and keep records. A cave dweller made little piles of stones to mark the boundaries of her land. A farmer made scratches on stones to mark the number of days since the full moon. Other scratches told a shepherd the number of skins a neighbor owed him. Villagers learned to communicate with distant places using a code of smoke signals or drumbeats. Hunters made pictures in sand and on the walls of caves.

From picture writing, called pictographs, the development of writing progressed in two ways. One, some of the pictures were simplified and given broader meanings. Thus, a person could write in pictures without having to draw realistically. The pictures became more abstract, a method similar to one that uses a stick figure to represent a human being. Two, a few designs were chosen from the pictographs and were used to represent the sounds of language, and these became an alphabet.

The development of pictures into letters made it possible for more people to learn to write and to read. This development also enabled people to write quickly. It made it easier for one generation to pass on its best ideas to the next generation. An alphabet allowed people far apart to communicate easily and clearly. The recording of the great history of Western civilization was made possible by the early development of alphabetic writing.

In terms of writing, the marks on paper are not important in themselves. They are important for what they represent and for the job they do. That job is to make it possible for people to communicate with each other. To communicate with someone means that you can share your information, experiences, and emotions with that person. Something in one person's mind is put into written symbols so that another can share it. Perhaps it appears in the form of a poem, which is to be read and enjoyed by many people. Perhaps it is only a person's note to a friend, asking for help.

Writing speaks for the writer; it represents his or her thinking. It can never be any better than the writer. If the writer is not thinking in a clear and organized manner, he or she will not write effectively. If the writer does not know the subject, his or her writing will show this ignorance.

Reading Time _____

Recalling Facts

1. Early villagers communicated with distant places by using
   - ☐ a. a code of drumbeats.
   - ☐ b. sand pictures.
   - ☐ c. piles of stones.

2. Pictographs are
   - ☐ a. smoke signals.
   - ☐ b. picture writing.
   - ☐ c. letters.

3. The development of pictures into letters resulted in
   - ☐ a. the alphabet.
   - ☐ b. Western civilization.
   - ☐ c. reading.

4. The alphabet represents
   - ☐ a. coded signals.
   - ☐ b. communication.
   - ☐ c. the sounds of language.

5. Written symbols enable people to
   - ☐ a. share information.
   - ☐ b. speak more clearly.
   - ☐ c. be honest.

Understanding Ideas

6. The symbol $, which stands for money, is an example of
   - ☐ a. a realistic picture.
   - ☐ b. a pictograph.
   - ☐ c. a letter.

7. The article wants you to understand that without communication,
   - ☐ a. writing is pointless.
   - ☐ b. people cannot think.
   - ☐ c. people could not share ideas.

8. It is likely that early cave drawings were made to
   - ☐ a. keep records or tell a story.
   - ☐ b. send messages to distant places.
   - ☐ c. develop an alphabet.

9. The article suggests that the importance of writing is dependent upon
   - ☐ a. whether it can be passed on to future generations.
   - ☐ b. how well it is written.
   - ☐ c. how well it communicates.

10. A successful computer manual was most likely written by
    - ☐ a. a person familiar with computers.
    - ☐ b. a person who is knowledgeable about art.
    - ☐ c. a person who is just learning about computers.

Correct Answers _____

An Ancient Empire

24

Ethiopia has historically been an empire, expanding in area and incorporating new groups into the population. A major expansion of the empire in the second half of the nineteenth century incorporated new peoples in the west, south, and east. The result is a population of great diversity.

Various religions are represented, with numerous people following Christianity, Islam, and traditional sects. Christianity was introduced into Ethiopia in the fourth century. It was the official state religion until 1974. Although there is often a great mix of religions in any given place, Christians tend to be the most numerous in highland areas. Muslims inhabit the lowlands. Traditional religious groups are found in the south and west.

According to estimates, the national population is about 54 million. It is most densely concentrated in the highland areas. Almost 90 percent of the people live outside cities. More than 45 percent of the people are 15 years of age and younger. Both birth and death rates are high. The average life expectancy at birth is about 45 years for males and 49 years for females, among the world's lowest.

The Ethiopian economy is one of poverty. Average annual incomes are estimated at between 100 and 150 dollars per person in United States dollars. Little is produced that is not needed within the country. Most people work as farmers or herders. Traditionally, farmers have worked small, scattered plots and have low harvests. Until 1974, most Ethiopians worked the land as tenants, as members of a community, or as private owners. The government officially took ownership of all land in 1975. All farming families were allotted a parcel of land, but they did not own it nor could they sell it. Throughout most of Ethiopia, there is mixed farming, the raising of both plants and animals. In most areas, the major crops include grains. In the southern half of the country, an additional main crop is ensete, a banana-like plant whose starchy stem is eaten rather than the fruit. Animals raised include cattle, sheep, goats, donkeys, mules, horses, camels, and chickens.

There are some areas with large commercial farms. Their products go largely to Ethiopian urban markets or international trade. When the government took the land, these farms were converted to collective, or state, farms. Their significant crops include sugar cane, cotton, and fruits from the north. Sesame, sorghum, and grains are grown in the south.

Reading Time _____

Recalling Facts

1. Until 1974, the official state religion in Ethiopia was
   - ☐ a. Christianity.
   - ☐ b. Judaism.
   - ☐ c. Islam.

2. Most of the people in Ethiopia live
   - ☐ a. in lowland areas.
   - ☐ b. in cities.
   - ☐ c. outside cities.

3. The average life expectancy in Ethiopia is
   - ☐ a. among the world's highest.
   - ☐ b. the world's lowest.
   - ☐ c. among the world's lowest.

4. All land in Ethiopia is owned by
   - ☐ a. large corporations.
   - ☐ b. the government.
   - ☐ c. private owners.

5. Average annual income per person in Ethiopia is
   - ☐ a. under 150 dollars.
   - ☐ b. between 150 and 200 dollars.
   - ☐ c. about 250 dollars.

Understanding Ideas

6. Life expectancy in Ethiopia is under 50 years of age, which suggests that
   - ☐ a. most Ethiopians die of old age.
   - ☐ b. living conditions are poor.
   - ☐ c. there is a food shortage.

7. The government in Ethiopia could be described as
   - ☐ a. powerful.
   - ☐ b. democratic.
   - ☐ c. weak.

8. Ethiopia needs most of what it produces, which suggests that
   - ☐ a. Ethiopia is a center of international trade.
   - ☐ b. imports exceed exports.
   - ☐ c. exports exceed imports.

9. It is likely that the education level of the typical Ethiopian is
   - ☐ a. high.
   - ☐ b. low.
   - ☐ c. average.

10. You can conclude from the article that industry in Ethiopia is
    - ☐ a. highly developed.
    - ☐ b. a low priority.
    - ☐ c. probably minimal.

Correct Answers _____

The Great Whales

25

The great whales are the largest animals that have ever lived. No dinosaur, not even the giant apatosaurus, was as big. Many of the great whales are 50 feet (15 meters) long when fully grown, and some are much longer. The blue whale, the largest whale of all, often grows from 90 to 100 feet (27 to 30 meters) long.

Whales are not fish. They belong to the same group of animals as cows, lions, dogs, and people. Whales are mammals, and like all mammals, they breathe air. They are warm-blooded, give birth to live young, and nurse them with milk. All mammals are hairy, but the dark gray or black skins of whales have almost no hair. Only a few whiskers remain to show that their ancestors were once hairy animals.

These distant ancestors of whales were land animals. Of all the mammals that have returned from the land to live in the sea, such as seals, sea lions, walruses, and manatees, none is as fit as the whale for life in the water.

The great whales are completely streamlined and well suited to water life. Their tapering shape and smooth skin help them move through the water easily. Their bones are soft and spongy, making them light in weight and not very strong for their size. But, since the whale's heavy body is supported by water, a strong skeleton is not as important as it is for a land mammal.

The bones of the whale's short neck are fused together. This gives more support to the huge head, which may make up one-fourth of the entire whale's size. But it also means that the whale cannot turn its head. This may not be much of a loss, since the whale's eyes are small and are set far back. Whales cannot see straight ahead. When they dive below 500 feet (152 meters), there is practically no light anyway.

Whales have lost the hind limbs their ancestors once had. Only a few small bones remain inside their bodies near the backbone. The front legs or arms have changed to become flippers, which the whale uses in balancing and steering. Instead of a tail, a whale has a pair of huge, thin, flattened flukes. They are horizontal and move up and down. The flukes are the whale's propeller. The up-and-down motion moves a great whale through the water.

Reading Time _____

Recalling Facts

1. The largest whale is the
   - ☐ a. blue whale.
   - ☐ b. gray whale.
   - ☐ c. white whale.

2. Like other mammals, whales
   - ☐ a. have fins.
   - ☐ b. are warm-blooded.
   - ☐ c. do not have hair.

3. Instead of a tail, a whale has
   - ☐ a. legs.
   - ☐ b. flukes.
   - ☐ c. flippers.

4. The whale's heavy body is supported by
   - ☐ a. its skeleton.
   - ☐ b. air pockets.
   - ☐ c. water.

5. Because its neck bones are fused, the whale
   - ☐ a. can only see what is directly in front of it.
   - ☐ b. cannot see in the dark.
   - ☐ c. cannot turn its head.

Understanding Ideas

6. You can conclude from the article that whales
   - ☐ a. can stay under water longer than any other mammal.
   - ☐ b. must surface in order to breathe.
   - ☐ c. breathe by finding underwater air pockets.

7. If a whale was placed on land, it is likely that
   - ☐ a. its skeleton would not support its weight.
   - ☐ b. it would weigh more than it does in the water.
   - ☐ c. its body would appear larger.

8. You can conclude that a whale's sense of sight is
   - ☐ a. very important.
   - ☐ b. more important than hearing.
   - ☐ c. not very important.

9. You can conclude that in order to live in the water, the whale
   - ☐ a. grew larger in size.
   - ☐ b. had to learn to swim.
   - ☐ c. changed physically.

10. It is likely that whales will
    - ☐ a. remain water mammals.
    - ☐ b. return to land once again.
    - ☐ c. eventually become fish.

Correct Answers _____

The Making of a Jet

26

The research, design, and production of airplanes, missiles, and spacecraft make up the aerospace industry. It is a relatively young industry. Its birthplace was the bicycle shop of Orville and Wilbur Wright in Dayton, Ohio. They built the first successful airplane, which they tested in December 1903. Today an aerospace manufacturing plant resembles a small city. Its offices, warehouses, factories, and other buildings may stretch for blocks.

A jet airplane has many thousands of parts. Therefore, it takes at least four or five years to start, develop, and produce one. Research and development, including engineering and testing, take place before manufacturing. Military or business leaders first specify the characteristics of the vehicle they want built. In a military plane fast takeoff, supersonic speed, armament, and bomb load are important. In a commercial airliner the number of passengers and cargo weight come first. Manufacturers of aerospace vehicles often develop their own designs.

The engineering department may have a thousand specialists. They prepare drawings that show the general outlines of the vehicle. Scale models are made for testing in a wind tunnel. Next a full-sized mock-up is built. Draftsmen then draw blueprints; a medium-sized jet plane may require up to 18,000 blueprints. Finally, an experimental model, or prototype, is constructed. Test pilots prove its airworthiness in actual flight.

The production of the vehicle takes careful planning. Plant layout experts make a miniature scale model of the plant to solve production problems. Contracts are assigned to subcontractors who will supply the parts. Workers must be trained. Machines, tools, fixtures, and jigs are ordered. Fixtures are devices for holding parts during machining or assembly. A jig is a device for guiding a tool, such as a drill. Metal parts are anodized to give them a tough, thin film that prevents corrosion and bonds paint. They are heat-treated to make them stronger and sprayed with paint to protect them.

When production begins, the factory is noisy and busy. Workers use riveting guns, mechanical hammers, saws, and many other tools. Overhead cranes carry materials. Tractors, trailers, and lift trucks move supplies.

The aerospace industry has borrowed the assembly-line method from the automobile makers. As the vehicle moves down the line, assemblers, riveters, and welders fit sections to it—the nose, fuselage, wings, tail, engines, and so on—until the craft is completed and ready for its test flight.

Reading Time _____

Recalling Facts

1. The aerospace industry
   - ☐ a. began during Roman times.
   - ☐ b. is more than 100 years old.
   - ☐ c. is 200 years old.

2. The first successful airplane was built
   - ☐ a. by the Orville brothers.
   - ☐ b. in Colorado.
   - ☐ c. by the Wright brothers.

3. After a mock-up of an airplane is built,
   - ☐ a. pilots test the vehicle.
   - ☐ b. various designs are considered.
   - ☐ c. draftsmen draw blueprints.

4. Airplanes are put together
   - ☐ a. one at a time.
   - ☐ b. on an assembly line.
   - ☐ c. by computers.

5. To prevent corrosion, metal parts are
   - ☐ a. painted.
   - ☐ b. heat-treated.
   - ☐ c. anodized.

Understanding Ideas

6. The article wants you to understand that the making of a jet
   - ☐ a. requires a small, but well-organized team.
   - ☐ b. requires years of detailed planning, development, and production.
   - ☐ c. is primarily the responsibility of engineers.

7. You can conclude from the article that military and passenger aircraft
   - ☐ a. are essentially built from the same designs.
   - ☐ b. are designed to suit the special needs of each type of craft.
   - ☐ c. have similar characteristics.

8. You can conclude from the article that the assembly-line method of airplane production is
   - ☐ a. the most efficient and cost-effective method.
   - ☐ b. the safest way.
   - ☐ c. more suitable for producing cars than airplanes.

9. It is likely that drawings and models of airplanes to be built serve to
   - ☐ a. solve problems at the earliest possible stages.
   - ☐ b. provide more jobs for researchers.
   - ☐ c. increase production speed on the assembly line.

10. Test-flying is important because
    - ☐ a. possible mistakes in design or production can be discovered.
    - ☐ b. an airplane is only as good as the pilot who flies it.
    - ☐ c. safety standards must be met.

Correct Answers _____

Gators and Crocs

27

The word *crocodilian* refers to both the alligator and the crocodile. Crocodilians are reptilian predators that are active mostly at night and usually live in water. During the day, they often lie at the water's edge, sunning themselves. At night, they retreat to the water. They live solitary lives and establish individual territories. A resident animal roars loudly at the approach of an intruder.

Young crocodiles and alligators eat worms and insects. As they mature, they add frogs, tadpoles, and fishes to their diets. Older animals eat mostly small animals, but some have even occasionally attacked humans. Crocodilians capture water animals in their jaws. To catch land animals, they knock unsuspecting prey into the water with their long, powerful tails. Animals too large to be swallowed whole are either torn to pieces or are drowned and permitted to decay in burrows. These burrows, which are dug at or just above the waterline, can extend for many feet and eventually end in a den, or chamber. The alligators hibernate in these burrows during cold weather.

Crocodilians draw strong reactions from their human neighbors, who have worshipped, feared, hunted, and tamed them for thousands of years. Ancient Egyptians considered the crocodile a symbol of the gods. Crocodiles are still regarded as sacred by some groups in Pakistan.

Crocodiles and alligators have been hunted for many reasons. The protection of domestic animals and the safety of humans are two reasons. Crocodiles are more likely to attack than are alligators, although alligators will attack when cornered. Humans kill thousands of crocodilians every year for sport and for commercial uses. Their skins provide leather for handbags, luggage, shoes, and belts. Alligators and crocodiles have also become pets and zoo specimens. If kept in captivity from birth, some learn to recognize their keepers, to beg for food, and to permit petting. Also, alligators and crocodiles have been bred and raised on farms to be harvested like other livestock.

The unrestricted hunting of crocodilians has severely depleted their population. The Chinese alligator is now considered rare. The disappearance of the crocodiles from parts of Africa has had a clear effect on the ecosystem. It has resulted in an overabundance of catfish. This, in turn, has greatly diminished the supply of other fishes. The American alligator has been on the increase since the Endangered Species Act gave it protection. Other governments also have passed laws to prevent the extinction of alligators and crocodiles.

Reading Time _____

Recalling Facts

1. The word *crocodilian* refers to
   - ☐ a. alligators and crocodiles.
   - ☐ b. alligators.
   - ☐ c. crocodiles.

2. Young crocodiles and alligators eat
   - ☐ a. fishes.
   - ☐ b. worms and insects.
   - ☐ c. plants.

3. The number of crocodiles and alligators
   - ☐ a. has greatly increased.
   - ☐ b. has greatly decreased.
   - ☐ c. is in the millions.

4. Ancient Egyptians thought of the crocodile as
   - ☐ a. an annoying pest.
   - ☐ b. a pet.
   - ☐ c. a symbol of the gods.

5. The American alligator is considered
   - ☐ a. the most dangerous alligator.
   - ☐ b. an endangered species.
   - ☐ c. to no longer exist.

Understanding Ideas

6. The greatest danger to crocodilians is from
   - ☐ a. starvation.
   - ☐ b. each other.
   - ☐ c. humans.

7. The article suggests that crocodilians
   - ☐ a. should be hunted only for food.
   - ☐ b. should not be hunted.
   - ☐ c. need protection.

8. The extinction of alligators and crocodiles would result in
   - ☐ a. an imbalance of the ecosystem.
   - ☐ b. the enactment of new laws.
   - ☐ c. a more equitable distribution of fish.

9. The skins of crocodilians make them
   - ☐ a. commercially valuable.
   - ☐ b. good animals for sport hunting.
   - ☐ c. excellent pets.

10. Crocodilians are bred and raised on farms so that
    - ☐ a. those in the wild can be protected.
    - ☐ b. they can be used for commercial purposes.
    - ☐ c. humans will feel safer.

Correct Answers _____

How Clothing Is Made

28

Cloth is used for more garments than any other material. There are three basic types of finished cloth—woven, knitted, and nonwoven. Woven cloth is the most widely used, but it is easier to produce a patterned cloth by knitting. The fibers of nonwoven cloth are bonded to a backing or locked together. Nonwoven fabrics may be created by using heat, mechanical energy, or chemicals.

The companies that produce finished cloth make up the textile industry. Most textiles in the United States are made in the South. The majority of these are exported for clothing manufacture in many other nations. Many garments are also made in the United States from materials imported from other countries.

Japan and the Netherlands also have large textile industries and sizable foreign markets. Most of the textiles that France produces are sold within the country. France neither imports nor exports much cloth. Textile industries have been established in a number of developing nations. Among them are Nigeria and Sudan.

Just as fibers are woven into finished cloth before garments can be made from them, other materials must also be processed before they can be made into clothing. Animal skins are treated by a chemical process called tanning to make soft and pliable leather. Furs may be let out, or cut into small pieces and re-sewn into a long, narrow strip. Latex must be converted into finished rubber.

Many steps are involved in producing an article of clothing. Some of these steps may be taken even before the processed material reaches the clothing factory. First a designer makes a sketch of the garment. From that sketch a sample is made to see if the style is practical. If the style is approved, a pattern is cut. Then the pattern must be remade in several different sizes.

The pieces of a pattern are placed on many layers of cloth for cutting. The worker who cuts out a pattern uses an electric knife that can slice through many thicknesses of cloth at once. After they have been cut, all the pieces of a garment are tied together according to size and passed on to a worker who sews them. Many different operators may work on a garment before it is completed.

Finished items of clothing are pressed, tagged, inspected, and packaged. Then they are shipped to the stores that will sell them. They may be transported by truck, train, ship, or airplane.

Reading Time _____

Recalling Facts

1. Most garments are made of
   - ☐ a. paper.
   - ☐ b. cloth.
   - ☐ c. chemicals.

2. Animal skins are made soft and pliable by a process called
   - ☐ a. stretching.
   - ☐ b. tanning.
   - ☐ c. soaking.

3. The first step in making a garment is
   - ☐ a. the designer's sketch.
   - ☐ b. a sample product.
   - ☐ c. cutting the pattern.

4. Before garments can be made from them, fibers must be
   - ☐ a. chemically treated.
   - ☐ b. let out.
   - ☐ c. woven into cloth.

5. Cloth is cut for clothing according to a
   - ☐ a. formula.
   - ☐ b. photograph.
   - ☐ c. pattern.

Understanding Ideas

6. A textile can be defined as
   - ☐ a. clothing.
   - ☐ b. a manufacturing company.
   - ☐ c. finished cloth.

7. From the article, you can conclude that clothing manufactured in the United States is made from materials
   - ☐ a. produced in the United States and in other countries.
   - ☐ b. exported from France.
   - ☐ c. sold within the country.

8. From the article you can conclude that because France neither exports nor imports much cloth,
   - ☐ a. clothing in France is made of leather, fur, and rubber.
   - ☐ b. France produces as much cloth as it needs.
   - ☐ c. French clothing designers and manufacturers dislike non-French cloth.

9. Patterns are cut from many thicknesses of cloth at once to
   - ☐ a. save time.
   - ☐ b. make cutting easier.
   - ☐ c. produce different sizes.

10. You can conclude from the article that the textile industry uses machines to make clothing because
    - ☐ a. the finished product is better.
    - ☐ b. machines are fast and cheap.
    - ☐ c. people are lazy.

Correct Answers _____

Paints

29

The most important material with which a painter works is the paint. Paints contain coloring matter called pigment. Most pigments are colors produced from plants, soil, or minerals. Today an increasing number of pigments are chemically produced.

Each kind of paint has unique qualities and can produce some effects but not others. The artist must work within the possibilities and limits of the materials.

In medieval times most artists worked with tempera. Tempera is made with earth or mineral pigments moistened with water and then mixed with an albumen. An albumen is a water-soluble protein substance, such as egg whites, that thickens when heated. Tempera color is flat and slightly glossy. Because it dries quickly, it cannot be used to model or vary surfaces. Tempera is usually painted on wood that has been covered with plaster and worked to a smooth, hard surface.

Fresco is a process of painting with water-soluble pigments on wet plaster. It is especially well-suited to large wall surfaces. The design of the painting is first sketched on the wall. At the beginning of each day's work, fresh plaster is applied. In the process of drying, the pigment combines with the plaster and becomes permanent. Colors, however, are somewhat limited.

Oil paints were first used in the early 1400s. Oil paint has since become the most commonly used of all mediums. The pigments are mixed with linseed oil, which allows them to spread thinly and easily. Oil paints can be made transparent or opaque so that the artist can control the depth of effect. Paintings in oil have extraordinary brilliance and depth.

Plastic compounds such as acrylic emulsions have been widely used since the mid-20th century. Some painters prefer them to oils because they dry faster and can be thinned with water. In addition, they are said to be more durable.

Watercolors, used in the East for many centuries, have been in use by Western artists for only a few hundred years. The most common type is transparent, allowing the paper on which it is applied to show through. Because watercolors are soluble in water, a great range of values is possible, from very light to very dark. Brilliant effects are possible, and watercolors have a fresh and spontaneous quality. Unlike oil paintings, which can be changed and worked on over a long period of time, watercolors are deadened when they are reworked.

Reading Time _____

Recalling Facts

1. Paint contains coloring matter called
   - ☐ a. pigment.
   - ☐ b. albumen.
   - ☐ c. plaster.

2. Most pigments are produced from
   - ☐ a. linseed oil.
   - ☐ b. plants, soil, or minerals.
   - ☐ c. eggs whites and water.

3. Tempera is made with
   - ☐ a. plaster and chemical pigments.
   - ☐ b. transparent pigments.
   - ☐ c. earth or mineral pigments and an albumen.

4. Fresco is
   - ☐ a. a process of painting on wet plaster.
   - ☐ b. a quick-drying flat paint medium.
   - ☐ c. the most commonly used of all mediums.

5. Oil paints have been in use
   - ☐ a. since the early 1400s.
   - ☐ b. since medieval times.
   - ☐ c. for only a few hundred years.

Understanding Ideas

6. The basic difference between oil paints and the other paints mentioned in this article is that oil paints
   - ☐ a. are not water soluble.
   - ☐ b. dry more quickly.
   - ☐ c. have been in use longer.

7. If you want to have great control over the depth of your painting, the best paint to use is
   - ☐ a. tempera.
   - ☐ b. oil.
   - ☐ c. watercolor.

8. If you want your painting to withstand frequent handling, the best paint to use is
   - ☐ a. tempera.
   - ☐ b. acrylic.
   - ☐ c. oil.

9. If you want to achieve a flat effect in your painting, the best paint to use is
   - ☐ a. oil.
   - ☐ b. tempera.
   - ☐ c. transparent watercolor.

10. The article wants you to understand that, when choosing a paint medium,
    - ☐ a. color and drying time are the most important considerations.
    - ☐ b. different paints are suited to different approaches and effects.
    - ☐ c. the water-soluble paints are always the best choice.

Correct Answers _____

Early Civilization

30

The earliest known urban culture on the Indian subcontinent existed in the Indus Valley from about 2500 BC to about 1700 BC. The earliest human settlements in the area were on the Pakistan-Iran border. They date from the late Stone Age. These settlements probably began in about 4000 BC. The people who lived in them led a semi-nomadic existence. They herded animals from one place to another and grew some food.

Sometime in the third millennium, increased population led to an eastward migration to the Valley. It is a floodplain, much like the Nile region of Egypt. The annual flooding brought deposits of silt. The soil was good for growing food and other crops with a minimum of labor and tools. The first settlements were probably established near the Indus Delta in the south. Later ones developed as civilization spread north and east.

The early centuries of settlement appear to have been a time of rapid population increase. The expansion resulted, in spite of the many different settlements, in a fairly uniform culture and a strong measure of economic and political control. The civil government in the leading cities was probably under the control of a class of priests or priest-kings, as in Egypt.

The animals raised by the Indus civilization were humped cattle, buffalo, sheep, goats, pigs, camels, dogs, cats, and domestic fowl. Elephants were also in the region. They may also have been domesticated.

Excavations of the Indus cities have produced evidence of a high level of artistic activity. There are a number of stone sculptures, cast-bronze figures, and terra-cotta figurines. Most of these are unclothed females heavily laden with jewelry. A few standing males have also been discovered. The figurines probably represent gods and goddesses, but many, such as animals and carts, are toys. It appears that the only painting was that done on pottery.

The religious beliefs of the Indus society are mostly a matter of conjecture. Buildings believed to be temples have been excavated. There were also animal cults devoted to the bull, the buffalo, and the tiger. Excavations at burial sites indicate belief in an afterlife: Household goods buried with bodies suggest the hope that the individuals would later need them.

The uniform civilization of the Indus Valley came to an end in about 1700 BC. Whether this was due to a major invasion, gradual incursion by outsiders, or other factors is unknown.

Reading Time _____

Recalling Facts

1. The earliest human settlers in the region lived
   - ☐ a. permanently in one place.
   - ☐ b. semi-nomadic lives.
   - ☐ c. in mud houses.

2. Most of the figurines excavated in the Indus Valley are
   - ☐ a. male.
   - ☐ b. female.
   - ☐ c. animals.

3. The religion of the Indus society
   - ☐ a. is mostly a matter of conjecture.
   - ☐ b. was probably Christian.
   - ☐ c. changed with the seasons.

4. The Indus civilization consisted of
   - ☐ a. one main settlement.
   - ☐ b. many different settlements.
   - ☐ c. nomadic tribes.

5. The end of the uniform civilization of the Indus Valley was caused by
   - ☐ a. a major invasion.
   - ☐ b. massive flooding.
   - ☐ c. unknown factors.

Understanding Ideas

6. The late Stone Age settlements that began in about 4000 BC
   - ☐ a. were more advanced than the Indus Valley settlements.
   - ☐ b. were established later than the Indus Valley settlements.
   - ☐ c. may have served as models for the Indus Valley settlements.

7. You can conclude from the article that religion
   - ☐ a. was not very important in the Indus civilization.
   - ☐ b. in Indus society decreased in importance as time passed.
   - ☐ c. was an important part of Indus civilization.

8. People living in the Indus Valley may have regarded painting as a
   - ☐ a. waste of time.
   - ☐ b. means of decoration.
   - ☐ c. high form of artistic expression.

9. Knowledge of the Indus civilization comes largely from
   - ☐ a. books.
   - ☐ b. archaeological digs.
   - ☐ c. cave paintings.

10. It is likely that early peoples settled in river valleys with rich soil because they
    - ☐ a. depended on crops for food.
    - ☐ b. needed special soil for building.
    - ☐ c. enjoyed living near the water.

Correct Answers _____

Ships of the Desert

31

For thousands of years, the camel has helped people live in the deserts of Asia and Africa. It can travel great distances over hot sands for days without water. It can carry a person or a load of freight. For this reason, it is sometimes called the "ship of the desert."

The camel supplies food and many valuable materials to desert dwellers. These people can live for many weeks on thick, cheesy camel's milk and on the meat of young camels. Desert dwellers make camel's hair into tents, blankets, rugs, clothing, and rope and cord. Dried camel droppings supply fuel for cooking fires. When a camel dies, its hide is used for making sandals, water bags, and many other necessities.

There are two kinds of camels. The dromedary, or Arabian, camel has a single hump on its back. The Asian camel has two humps. The dromedary once roamed wild but is now found only in domestication. Groups of them, however, are often left on their own for up to five months. The Asian camel is primarily a domesticated animal, but small wild herds are still found in areas of Mongolia and China. Only about 300 to 500 Asian camels still live in a wild state, so the species is considered in danger of extinction.

Although often ill-tempered, the camel is wonderfully adapted for the work it has to do. No other animal can live and work on such scant supplies of food and water in so hot and dry a climate.

One of the few things that a camel will do on command is kneel. It is easier for a person to climb onto or load up the animal when it kneels. The camel seldom works without a protest. The uproar in a camel yard when a caravan is being loaded is deafening.

The camel's most striking feature is the large hump or humps on its back. The hump is formed from fat and muscle. When a camel is well fed and given enough water, the hump is erect. If the camel has to go without food and water for a period of time, the hump becomes limp and leans to one side.

The camel's body is covered with a shaggy, sand-colored coat. The hair sheds in great handfuls, giving the animal a perpetually frowsy look. Long eyelashes protect the eyes from sandstorms and the glare of the desert sun.

Reading Time _____

Recalling Facts

1. Items such as tents, rugs, and rope are made from camel
   - ☐ a. hair.
   - ☐ b. hides.
   - ☐ c. droppings.

2. A two-humped camel is called
   - ☐ a. an Asian camel.
   - ☐ b. a dromedary.
   - ☐ c. a domesticated camel.

3. Camels are known for their
   - ☐ a. obedience.
   - ☐ b. good nature.
   - ☐ c. ill temper.

4. On command, a camel will
   - ☐ a. run.
   - ☐ b. kneel.
   - ☐ c. work.

5. Today most camels are
   - ☐ a. found in the wild.
   - ☐ b. domesticated.
   - ☐ c. found in zoos.

Understanding Ideas

6. Camels are called "ships of the desert" because of their
   - ☐ a. resemblance to large ships.
   - ☐ b. ability to go without water.
   - ☐ c. usefulness as transportation.

7. The number of Asian camels is
   - ☐ a. greater than the number of Arabian camels.
   - ☐ b. about the same as the number of Arabian camels.
   - ☐ c. less than the number of Arabian camels.

8. You can conclude from the article that a camel's hump
   - ☐ a. serves no special function.
   - ☐ b. stores food and water.
   - ☐ c. makes it ill tempered.

9. It is likely that in a non-desert climate, the camel would be regarded as
   - ☐ a. a popular means of transportation.
   - ☐ b. an unpopular means of transportation.
   - ☐ c. an ideal substitute for a horse.

10. You can conclude that a camel's height is usually
    - ☐ a. greater than a human's.
    - ☐ b. less than a human's.
    - ☐ c. about the same as a human's.

Correct Answers _____

Sicily

32

Sicily is the largest and most populous island in the Mediterranean Sea. It forms an autonomous region of Italy with several other islands. At the northeastern corner of the island, the Strait of Messina separates it from mainland Italy. Its strategic location gives Sicily command of sea and air routes between southern Europe and Africa. Palermo, the capital and largest city, is a center for trade, commerce, and industry.

Mountains cover most of the northern part of the island. Flat landscape is found only along the coast. With intense volcanic activity, Sicily is subject to severe earthquakes. Mount Etna, the island's highest peak, is also Europe's largest active volcano. Winter rainfall ranges from about 20 inches (50 centimeters) on the plains to 50 inches (130 centimeters) in the mountains. Summers are dry and hot. Once covered with trees, the island is now less than 4 percent forested. Cutting down forests for agriculture and other uses has caused severe soil-erosion problems. Attempts are being made to reforest the land.

Farming and livestock raising are the chief occupations in Sicily. More than three-fourths of the island is cultivated, but yields are low. Vineyards and orchards of lemon, orange, tangerine, and olive trees flourish on the lower mountain slopes. Wheat, barley, corn, almonds, grapes, and some cotton are produced. Cattle, mules, donkeys, and sheep are raised. Many peasants do not own their farms. The majority of agricultural land is privately owned.

Sicily's isolation and distance from mainland Italy accounts, in part, for its economic underdevelopment. In the last few decades, however, there has been a marked expansion of heavy industries based on petroleum refining, natural gas, and chemicals. Other industries include salt extraction, wine making, textiles, shipbuilding and repair, fertilizers, and pharmaceuticals. Food-processing industries include vegetable and fish canning and the extraction of citric acid and essential oils. Sulfur mining, once Sicily's principal mining activity, has declined. Almonds, fruits, tomatoes, artichokes, and fish are major exports.

Sicily was colonized by the Greeks during the eighth century BC. In the third century BC, it became the first Roman province. Large quantities of grain were produced and sent to Italy. Normans conquered Sicily in the eleventh century. It was ruled by the House of Bourbon during the 1700s and 1800s. It also became a major center of revolutionary movements in the nineteenth century. In 1861, it was incorporated into the United Kingdom of Italy.

Reading Time _____

Recalling Facts

1. Sicily is located in
   - ☐ a. the Mediterranean Sea.
   - ☐ b. the northern corner of Italy.
   - ☐ c. the Atlantic Ocean.

2. Europe's largest active volcano is
   - ☐ a. Sicily.
   - ☐ b. Mount Etna.
   - ☐ c. Palermo.

3. Sicily's severe soil-erosion problems are mainly the result of
   - ☐ a. dry, hot weather.
   - ☐ b. volcanic activity.
   - ☐ c. felling forests.

4. Chief occupations in Sicily are
   - ☐ a. mining and shipbuilding.
   - ☐ b. wine making and fishing.
   - ☐ c. farming and livestock raising.

5. Sicily's first colonists were
   - ☐ a. Greek.
   - ☐ b. Roman.
   - ☐ c. Norman.

Understanding Ideas

6. The article wants you to understand that
   - ☐ a. Sicily will soon solve its problems.
   - ☐ b. Sicily suffers from many problems.
   - ☐ c. Sicily's problems are the result of its location.

7. The expansion of industries in Sicily will most likely
   - ☐ a. drain Sicily's resources.
   - ☐ b. interfere with development.
   - ☐ c. improve the island's economy.

8. You can conclude from the article that earthquake and volcano activity on Sicily
   - ☐ a. accounts for Sicily's isolation from mainland Italy.
   - ☐ b. is likely a hindrance to Sicily's development.
   - ☐ c. attracts tourists.

9. Palermo's reputation as a center of trade, commerce, and industry is no doubt due to
   - ☐ a. Sicily's government.
   - ☐ b. Sicily's location.
   - ☐ c. its population.

10. Three-fourths of Sicily is cultivated, but yields are low, which suggests that
    - ☐ a. better farming methods are needed.
    - ☐ b. farmers should work harder.
    - ☐ c. more land should be cultivated.

Correct Answers _____

The Start of Language

33

*L*anguage can be defined as a system of sounds, signs, and gestures that represent the same things to all members of a group. These utterances are used to represent things whether or not the things they represent are present.

Symbolic language is considered a human skill. The language of animals is considered direct and very simple in comparison. It is thought to consist of responses to what can be detected by the senses. When a dog barks at a stranger, it is responding to the presence of the stranger. It cannot express its attitude toward strangers without a stranger at hand. Dogs appear capable of expressing only a few basic ideas—hostility, affection, hunger, the desire to stay or go, and a few others. Like many other animals, dogs seem able to communicate only about the simplest matters and in concrete rather than abstract terms. If a dog wants to go outside, it may scratch a door or whine. It cannot, however, express reasons it may have for wanting to go out.

It is not known when humans first discovered the symbolic power of language. There are, however, theories about this discovery. Most involve imagining a simple coincidence of events: A primitive man digs for clams on a beach. As he digs, he makes sounds. At one point, he bites into an especially tasty clam. The next sound he makes he associates with the pleasant experience of taste. He points to the clam and makes the sound again, reinforcing the sound with a smile of pleasure. His companions understand. Thereafter, they have a sound to use for suggesting that it is time to go clam hunting or for telling someone they have found a good clam.

However language was discovered, it was probably something as simple as that. Humans gave names to the things around them, and to their feelings, beliefs, and actions. These were words. Humans then developed ways to join these words together into sentences. They became able to talk about the clams found on the seashore even when the clams and the seashore were not present. They became able to compose poems and to make speeches with such words. Most important, they became able to think with words. Human thinking would be very limited if they could only use remembered pictures to create and share ideas; abstract thinking and communication is made possible with language.

Reading Time _____

Recalling Facts

1. A system of sounds, signs, and gestures with shared meanings is called
   - ☐ a. abstract thinking.
   - ☐ b. language.
   - ☐ c. communication.

2. The language of animals is thought to consist of
   - ☐ a. responses to what can be detected by the senses.
   - ☐ b. instinctive gestures common to all animals.
   - ☐ c. abstract utterances.

3. Language can be used to represent a thing
   - ☐ a. only if that thing is present.
   - ☐ b. only if that thing is invisible.
   - ☐ c. whether or not that thing is present.

4. Most theories about how and when humans first discovered the symbolic power of language involve imagining a
   - ☐ a. long process in which humans mimicked animal language.
   - ☐ b. supernatural event that changed human history.
   - ☐ c. simple coincidence of events.

5. Names given to things, feelings, beliefs, and actions are called
   - ☐ a. definitions.
   - ☐ b. words.
   - ☐ c. songs.

Understanding Ideas

6. You can conclude from the article that
   - ☐ a. advanced thinking came before language.
   - ☐ b. language advanced human thinking.
   - ☐ c. without language, humans could not think.

7. The article suggests that human thinking
   - ☐ a. depends on language.
   - ☐ b. is more abstract because of language.
   - ☐ c. is limited by language.

8. Without words, recording ideas would be
   - ☐ a. impossible.
   - ☐ b. limited to pictures.
   - ☐ c. limited to scholars.

9. Sentences are
   - ☐ a. recognizable words joined together.
   - ☐ b. united feelings.
   - ☐ c. ideas joined by letters.

10. You can conclude from the article that
    - ☐ a. language was probably discovered by the Romans.
    - ☐ b. language is limited to humans.
    - ☐ c. no one knows how language was discovered.

Correct Answers _____

Alpine Life

34

From prehistoric times, the Alps have been the site of human habitation. German cultures generally developed in the eastern Alps. Roman culture influenced the West. The main language groups that survive today are German, French, and Italian. Romansh, an ancient Latin language, is spoken in a region of eastern Switzerland.

Some Alpine folk traditions are still preserved and often displayed as part of the tourist and entertainment industry. Alpine music, poetry, dance, woodcarving, and embroidery are quite distinctive. Yodeling, a kind of singing, is marked by rapid switching of the voice to and from falsetto. The alpenhorn, used for signaling between valleys, is a trumpet-like wooden instrument 5 to 14 feet (1.5 to 4 meters) long.

During the first five centuries of the Christian era, Rome dominated the Alps. The Romans built roads through the passes north and west to promote trade and link their Mediterranean and northern provinces. Economic activity of the period included wine grape culture, iron-ore mining, and pottery manufacture.

Alpine valleys and many mountainsides were cleared of forests during the Middle Ages. Farmers settled the land, planted crops, and developed transhumance. In this Alpine practice, cattle are stall-fed in the villages during the winter and led to high mountain meadows for summer grazing. While the animals are gone, the farm family tends hay, grain, and other forage crops for use in the winter. Milk produced in the summer is usually made into cheese. In the winter, it is sold to dairies. Forestry is practiced in the Alps, and forest conservation programs have been developed.

During the nineteenth century, railroads were constructed, opening up the area. Hydroelectricity was developed. The electric power made by damming Alpine rivers encouraged manufacturing. The region has no coal or oil. Industrial growth caused many people to leave agriculture and take factory jobs. Types of light manufacturing, from watches to precision machinery, have thrived in the Alps.

Tourism has become a major Alpine industry. Europe has prospered as air, auto, and rail transportation to the Alps improved. One of the world's longest auto tunnels, passing through Mont Blanc, was opened in 1965. Railroads follow paths along traditional routes and passes. Winter sports gained mass popularity as a result of the accessibility of the Alpine region. Today entire villages lodge, feed, and entertain tourists. Resorts such as Innsbruck, Grenoble, and St. Moritz are world famous. All of them have hosted Olympic winter games.

Reading Time _____

Recalling Facts

1. Romansh is
   - ☐ a. a type of German food.
   - ☐ b. an ancient Latin language.
   - ☐ c. an Alpine folk tradition.

2. A trumpet-like wooden instrument used for signaling in the Alps is called the
   - ☐ a. yodel.
   - ☐ b. glockenspiel.
   - ☐ c. alpenhorn.

3. One of the world's longest auto tunnels passes through
   - ☐ a. Innsbruck.
   - ☐ b. St. Moritz.
   - ☐ c. Mont Blanc.

4. In the Alps, tourism is
   - ☐ a. a major industry.
   - ☐ b. practically nonexistent.
   - ☐ c. the result of increased manufacturing.

5. Innsbruck, Grenoble, and St. Moritz are
   - ☐ a. farming centers.
   - ☐ b. former hosts of the Olympic winter games.
   - ☐ c. the world's tallest mountains.

Understanding Ideas

6. The Alpine region can be characterized as
   - ☐ a. a commercial center.
   - ☐ b. prosperous.
   - ☐ c. economically deprived.

7. Farming in the Alps is primarily
   - ☐ a. run by big businesses.
   - ☐ b. a family business.
   - ☐ c. a seasonal job.

8. You can conclude from the article that transhumance was developed as a result of
   - ☐ a. limited winter grazing for cattle.
   - ☐ b. an increase in the cattle population.
   - ☐ c. laws regarding the humane treatment of animals.

9. It is likely that the Alpine region would not have prospered without
   - ☐ a. the many improvements in transportation.
   - ☐ b. forest conservation.
   - ☐ c. the skiing industry.

10. You can conclude from the article that resorts in the Alpine region were chosen to host the Olympic winter games because
    - ☐ a. they are well-known to tourists.
    - ☐ b. Alpine folk traditions are preserved there.
    - ☐ c. of their ideal conditions for winter sports.

Correct Answers _____

Crabs

35

Crabs have flatter, broader bodies than do lobsters, crayfish, and shrimp. Their front legs have large pinching claws. In crabs that swim, the last pair of legs are broad and flattened, serving as paddles. Crabs' eyes are mounted on movable stalks. Crabs that live in water breathe by means of gills. Land crabs have modified gills that function as lungs. Some crabs feed on vegetable matter. Others eat small living animals. Most crabs, however, are scavengers, eating dead or decaying material.

Many different kinds of crabs live throughout the world. Most crabs live in the sea, on or near the bottom. Some crabs live on land, sometimes several miles from water. To lay their eggs, the females must return to the water. Ghost crabs stay on the ocean shore above the high-water line. Fiddler crabs are common along the Atlantic coast in areas of salt water. The male fiddler has an enlarged right claw that it waves back and forth as a signal to available females and to competing males. Fiddlers live in burrows in the sand or mud, where they stay during winter and high tides.

Most hermit crabs have long, soft abdomens that are spirally coiled. They occupy abandoned snail shells by thrusting the abdomen into the shell and holding onto it. They do not kill the original owner of the shell, though they will fight other hermit crabs to determine occupancy of a shell. The hermit crab drags the shell behind as it walks about. When the crab grows larger, it seeks a larger shell.

A common crab along the Atlantic and Gulf coasts of the United States is the blue crab. Blue crabs are swimming crabs that live in marine waters but also enter shallow brackish areas.

Crabs are an important food source. Some are canned and others are sold fresh to restaurants. In the United States, three main kinds of crabs are caught for their meat. Blue crabs are caught commercially in open water by trawls or are removed from the mud with dredges. Dungeness crabs are native to the Pacific coastlines of North America. King crabs, the largest crabs, come from the North Pacific and the Bering Sea. A single king crab can provide as much as five pounds (2.3 kilograms) of meat. Various kinds of stone, rock, and sand crabs are gathered along coasts for food, but they are not commercially important.

Reading Time _____

Recalling Facts

1. A crab's front legs
   - ☐ a. serve as paddles.
   - ☐ b. have large pinching claws.
   - ☐ c. have gills.

2. Crabs that live in water breathe by means of
   - ☐ a. lungs.
   - ☐ b. gills.
   - ☐ c. modified gills.

3. Most crabs live
   - ☐ a. on land.
   - ☐ b. in rivers and streams.
   - ☐ c. in the sea.

4. The largest crabs are called
   - ☐ a. blue crabs.
   - ☐ b. king crabs.
   - ☐ c. dinosaur crabs.

5. Fiddler crabs live in
   - ☐ a. deep water.
   - ☐ b. snail shells.
   - ☐ c. sand or mud.

Understanding Ideas

6. Swimming crabs have broad, flattened rear legs, which
   - ☐ a. help them swim more efficiently.
   - ☐ b. help them breathe.
   - ☐ c. aid in jumping.

7. A crab's large, pinching claws would likely be useful for
   - ☐ a. walking.
   - ☐ b. capturing food.
   - ☐ c. breathing.

8. You can conclude from the article that a hermit crab lives in an empty snail shell
   - ☐ a. to protect its long, soft abdomen.
   - ☐ b. because it feeds on snails.
   - ☐ c. to deposit eggs.

9. Fiddler crabs probably got their name from
   - ☐ a. where they live.
   - ☐ b. the sound they make while burrowing.
   - ☐ c. their habit of waving their large right claw.

10. It is likely that the differences among crabs are a result of
   - ☐ a. their need to adapt to their environment.
   - ☐ b. their choice of food.
   - ☐ c. different fishing techniques.

Correct Answers _____

The Worst of Pests

36

The cockroach is one of the most obnoxious of household pests. This brown or black insect can be found in houses, apartment and office buildings, ships, trains, and airplanes in many parts of the world. Domestic cockroaches, which are also called roaches, have a disagreeable odor. They live in warm, dark areas. Their broad, flat bodies permit them to crawl in narrow cracks and along pipes. They hide in the daytime, coming out at night to feed. The diet of the cockroach, which includes both plant and animal products, ranges from food, paper, clothing, and books to dead insects. Cockroaches can be difficult to eliminate entirely, but a variety of common poisons and traps are effective in controlling their numbers. They are thought to transmit several human diseases.

Cockroaches are among the oldest living insects. Fossil cockroaches that resemble today's species have been found in Coal Age deposits more than 320 million years old. About 3,500 species have been identified. Although the most pesky are those that infest households in the temperate regions, most species are tropical. Some reach lengths of several inches, and many are colorful. Several species of woodland cockroaches are found in temperate regions. These live amid decaying wood and other vegetation and do not enter houses.

The cockroach has long, powerful legs and can run very fast. Long antennae on the head are used for feeling in dark places. Most species have two pairs of wings that are larger in the males. The female cockroach carries her eggs in a leathery capsule at the rear of the abdomen. Females of some common species lay 16 to 45 eggs at a time. The female deposits the eggs, which take from four to 12 weeks to hatch. Soft, white young called nymphs emerge from the eggs. After exposure to air, the nymphs harden and turn brown.

The German cockroach is a common household pest. It is light brown with two dark stripes just behind the head. Because it is only about half an inch (12.7 millimeters) long, it can easily enter or be transported into homes.

The American cockroach, also called a water bug, is long, reddish brown, and lives outdoors or in dark, heated indoor areas. Favorite places are basements and furnace rooms. This cockroach, a native of tropical and subtropical America, has well-developed wings and can fly long distances. Cockroaches are closely related to grasshoppers, katydids, and crickets.

Reading Time _____

Recalling Facts

1. Roaches live in areas that are
   - ☐ a. damp.
   - ☐ b. warm and dark.
   - ☐ c. cold.

2. The cockroach's long antennae on the head are used for
   - ☐ a. feeding.
   - ☐ b. feeling in dark places.
   - ☐ c. flying.

3. Young cockroaches are called
   - ☐ a. water bugs.
   - ☐ b. fossils.
   - ☐ c. nymphs.

4. Young cockroaches harden and turn brown when they
   - ☐ a. hatch.
   - ☐ b. are exposed to air.
   - ☐ c. mature.

5. Cockroaches feed
   - ☐ a. at night.
   - ☐ b. during the day.
   - ☐ c. every two days.

Understanding Ideas

6. Cockroaches would most likely prefer living
   - ☐ a. near an oven.
   - ☐ b. in a warm, sunny spot.
   - ☐ c. by the ocean.

7. The cockroach's diet is best described as
   - ☐ a. limited.
   - ☐ b. wide-ranging.
   - ☐ c. meat-eating.

8. One reason that cockroaches are difficult to eliminate entirely might be that
   - ☐ a. they are very adaptable.
   - ☐ b. they can run very fast.
   - ☐ c. they can fly long distances.

9. Humans should beware of cockroaches mainly because they
   - ☐ a. transmit diseases.
   - ☐ b. have a strong odor.
   - ☐ c. devour human food.

10. Cockroaches have survived for millions of years, which suggests that they
    - ☐ a. live a long time.
    - ☐ b. are able to adapt to changing environments.
    - ☐ c. are decreasing in number.

Correct Answers _____

Unit 2

Reading Rate

Instructions: Put an X on the line above each lesson number to show your reading time and words-per-minute rate for that lesson.

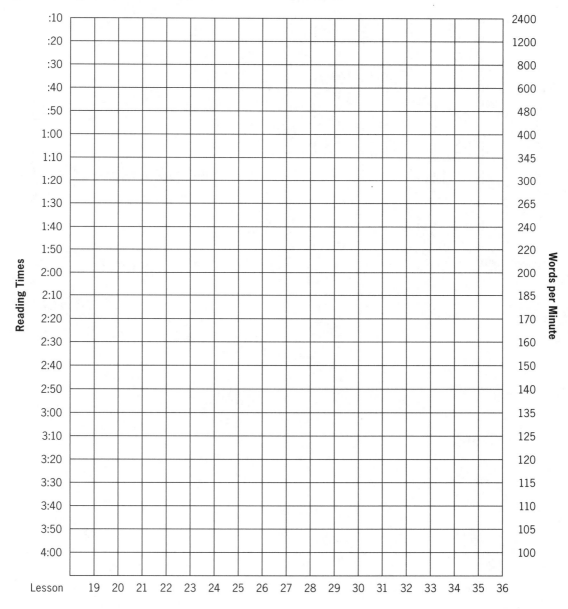

Reading Times		Words per Minute
:10		2400
:20		1200
:30		800
:40		600
:50		480
1:00		400
1:10		345
1:20		300
1:30		265
1:40		240
1:50		220
2:00		200
2:10		185
2:20		170
2:30		160
2:40		150
2:50		140
3:00		135
3:10		125
3:20		120
3:30		115
3:40		110
3:50		105
4:00		100

Lesson   19 20 21 22 23 24 25 26 27 28 29 30 31 32 33 34 35 36

Unit 2

Comprehension Score

Instructions: Put an X on the line above each lesson number to indicate your total correct answers and comprehension score for that lesson.

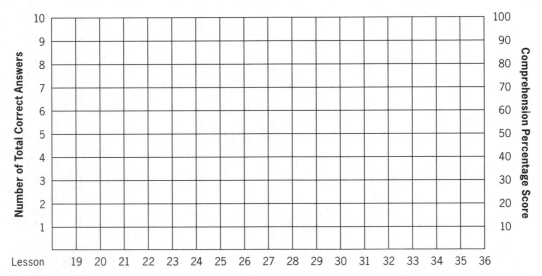

At Home in the Zoo

37

Nearly every child and adult enjoys the zoo, but what about the animals? Many people wonder if it is cruel to remove animals from their homes and confine them behind bars and trenches where thousands of human beings stare at them.

In certain ways animals may fare better in zoos than in their natural surroundings. Wild animals may be underfed. Some must roam far and wide to find sufficient food. Some wild animals suffer from wounds or disease. Most animals must be on guard constantly against enemies. After a few weeks in a zoo, the steady food supply, clean living quarters, and medical care often give rise to an improvement in the physical health and appearance of captive animals. Many mate and rear young in captivity. Many also seem to enjoy human visitors just as much as the visitors enjoy them.

Bears and seals, for example, love to show off for zoo visitors. Monkeys and apes also appear to enjoy human companionship, especially that of their keepers. The Lincoln Park Zoo in Chicago once tried using one-way glass in the monkey house. People could look in and see the monkeys, but the monkeys could not look out and see the people. The monkeys became unhappy, and the glass was removed. At once, the animals regained their lively spirits.

Visitors may mistake certain animal actions as signs of unhappiness. Endless pacing back and forth may be simply an animal's way of getting exercise. When brown bears pad the ground for hours, they are following an instinct to pack down snow, even though they have no snow to pack. If a monkey gazes longingly into space, is it wishing it was back in the jungle? It is probably just waiting for its food.

Most animals have a great need to feel secure. They want an area to claim as their territory, a place where they can hide and feel safe. On the rare occasions when an animal escapes from a zoo, it usually comes back to its quarters after a few hours or days, especially if it escapes into areas of human habitation. That world—so different from the animal's native habitat and from its zoo quarters—is likely terrifying. The animal returns to the place where it feels secure and where it can find food and water. Often the animals walk back through the open cage door of their own accord.

Reading Time _____

Recalling Facts

1. Animals in the wild
   - ☐ a. are better fed than animals in zoos.
   - ☐ b. are often without sufficient food.
   - ☐ c. are well fed.

2. Animals in captivity
   - ☐ a. never mate.
   - ☐ b. may mate and rear young.
   - ☐ c. must often fight to protect themselves.

3. Most animals have a great need for
   - ☐ a. security.
   - ☐ b. isolation.
   - ☐ c. freedom.

4. Living in the wild is dangerous for animals because of
   - ☐ a. natural enemies.
   - ☐ b. bad weather.
   - ☐ c. lack of shelter.

5. Animals that like to show off include
   - ☐ a. lions.
   - ☐ b. crocodiles.
   - ☐ c. seals.

Understanding Ideas

6. From the article you can conclude that animals in zoos
   - ☐ a. are healthier than animals in the wild.
   - ☐ b. miss their natural surroundings.
   - ☐ c. dislike being caged.

7. Monkeys placed behind one-way glass were unhappy, which suggests that monkeys
   - ☐ a. like their privacy.
   - ☐ b. are social creatures.
   - ☐ c. are afraid of glass.

8. According to the article, animal instinct
   - ☐ a. disappears in captive animals.
   - ☐ b. remains strong in captive animals.
   - ☐ c. is stronger in wild animals.

9. From the article you can conclude that animals
   - ☐ a. imitate human behavior.
   - ☐ b. behave according to instinct.
   - ☐ c. change their behavior in a zoo environment.

10. The article suggests that concern about the well-being of captive animals is
    - ☐ a. justified.
    - ☐ b. exaggerated.
    - ☐ c. not based on fact.

Correct Answers _____

Fire Extinguishers

38

S everal types of fire extinguishers have been invented to put out different kinds of fires. They must be ready for instant use when fires break out. Most portable kinds operate for less than a minute, so they are useful only for small fires. The law requires ships, trains, intercity buses, and airplanes to carry extinguishers. They hang in schools, theaters, factories, stores, and high-rise buildings. Some people keep them in their homes, barns, and automobiles.

Since fuel, oxygen, and heat must be present for fire to exist, one or more of these three elements must be removed or reduced to extinguish a fire. If the heat is reduced by cooling the substance below the kindling temperature, the fire goes out. The cooling method is the most common way to put out a fire. Water is the best cooling agent because it is low in cost and usually readily available.

Another method of extinguishing fire is by eliminating or diluting the oxygen. This is usually done by smothering or blanketing the fire. A substance that is not readily combustible is used to cover the fire. Sand, foam, steam, or a nonflammable chemical may be employed. A blanket or rug may be used to cover and smother a small blaze.

A third method is called separation. This method involves removing the fuel, or combustible material, from a fire. In forest fires, for instance, the trees may be cut away, leaving a fire lane in which the spreading flame can find no fuel. Explosives may be employed to block oil-well fires.

The method used to put out a fire depends on the type of fire. Fires have been grouped into three classes. Fires in wood, paper, cloth, and similar common materials are called Class A fires. These materials usually form glowing coals, which help to sustain the fire. Such fires can be stopped most readily by cooling with water or watery solutions.

Blazes in flammable liquids such as gasoline, oil, or grease are called Class B fires. The material and the fire would float and spread if a stream of water were used on the flames. Such blazes are smothered; that is, oxygen from the air is cut off. Class C fires—those in charged electrical equipment—should be put out by an agent that does not conduct electricity.

Reading Time _____

Recalling Facts

1. The most common way to put out a fire is by
   ☐ a. cooling.
   ☐ b. diluting the oxygen.
   ☐ c. removing the fuel.

2. The best cooling agent in putting out a fire is
   ☐ a. a blanket.
   ☐ b. gasoline.
   ☐ c. water.

3. The method that is used to put out a fire depends upon
   ☐ a. its location.
   ☐ b. the type of fire.
   ☐ c. the time of day.

4. A fire lane deprives a fire of
   ☐ a. oxygen.
   ☐ b. heat.
   ☐ c. fuel.

5. Fires are grouped into
   ☐ a. two classes.
   ☐ b. three classes.
   ☐ c. four classes.

Understanding Ideas

6. Large fires cannot be put out by portable fire extinguishers because the extinguishers
   ☐ a. contain the wrong kind of chemicals.
   ☐ b. do not contain enough chemicals.
   ☐ c. often malfunction.

7. You can conclude from the article that sand
   ☐ a. makes an excellent fuel.
   ☐ b. does not burn easily.
   ☐ c. is used in many fire extinguishers.

8. The cooling method is most often used to put out a fire, which suggests that most fires are
   ☐ a. Class A fires.
   ☐ b. Class B fires.
   ☐ c. Class C fires.

9. The most important element in fighting a fire is
   ☐ a. patience.
   ☐ b. education.
   ☐ c. speed.

10. Class A fires can be extinguished by
    ☐ a. cooling only.
    ☐ b. smothering only.
    ☐ c. cooling, smothering, or removing the fuel.

Correct Answers _____

FUSION Reading *Plus*

Anne Hutchinson, Religious Pioneer 39

Anne Hutchinson was one of the first New England colonists to challenge the authority of the Puritan leaders in religious matters. She preferred following her conscience over blind obedience. Her protest helped establish the principle of freedom of religion.

Anne Marbury was born in Alford, England, and baptized on July 20, 1591. Her father, an English clergyman, was twice imprisoned for preaching against the established Church of England. Although Marbury had no formal education, she learned much by listening to her father and his friends discuss religion and government. When Marbury was 14, her father was appointed to St. Martin's Church in London. At 21, she married William Hutchinson, her childhood sweetheart, and they returned to Alford to live. They had 14 children. Despite her busy household, Hutchinson was active in religious affairs and often made the 24-mile (39-kilometer) journey to Boston, England, to hear John Cotton preach. In 1633, Cotton was compelled to leave England because of his Puritan sympathies. With Hutchinson's eldest son, Edward, he fled to New England. The Hutchinsons, with their other children, followed the next year and settled in Boston, Massachusetts.

Soon Hutchinson was holding weekly prayer meetings for the women of the colony. At these meetings, she often criticized the preaching of the clergy. She believed that the Lord dwelt within each individual, and she proclaimed that faith alone would attain salvation. This was in opposition to the teachings of the Puritan leaders. By 1636, she had recruited many converts, including her brother-in-law, the Reverend John Wheelwright, and the young governor, Henry Vane. John Cotton initially supported her but later publicly renounced her teachings.

With Governor Vane a convert, the other leaders feared civil disobedience and sought to regain control. When Vane returned to England in 1636, they obtained the governorship for John Winthrop. He banished Wheelwright to New Hampshire and brought Hutchinson to trial. She was banished in November 1637, but because of ill health was permitted to spend the winter in nearby Roxbury.

During the winter, Cotton and other clergy pressured Hutchinson to deny her beliefs. When she refused, she was excommunicated from the church. She and her family and friends moved to Rhode Island in 1638 and founded a new colony. After her husband's death in 1642, Hutchinson moved with her younger children to Pelham Bay in New York. In 1643, she and most of her family were killed by Native Americans.

Reading Time _____

Recalling Facts

1. Anne Hutchinson believed in
   - ☐ a. women's liberation.
   - ☐ b. religious freedom.
   - ☐ c. a strong central government.

2. Anne Hutchinson's father was
   - ☐ a. a teacher.
   - ☐ b. a politician.
   - ☐ c. a clergyman.

3. Anne Hutchinson believed that in order to attain salvation, people had to
   - ☐ a. follow the laws of the church.
   - ☐ b. have faith.
   - ☐ c. move to New England.

4. Originally, Anne Hutchinson was a follower of
   - ☐ a. John Cotton's Puritan beliefs.
   - ☐ b. the Church of England.
   - ☐ c. John Calvin.

5. As a result of her religious beliefs, Anne Hutchinson was
   - ☐ a. burned at the stake.
   - ☐ b. banished to a foreign country.
   - ☐ c. excommunicated from the church.

Understanding Ideas

6. It is likely that Anne Hutchinson's religious ideas were
   - ☐ a. very popular in England.
   - ☐ b. influenced by those of her father.
   - ☐ c. a result of her formal education.

7. You can conclude from the article that during Anne Hutchinson's time, women
   - ☐ a. were unlikely to be religious leaders.
   - ☐ b. often spoke out about their religious beliefs.
   - ☐ c. were against religious freedom.

8. You can conclude from the article that during Anne Hutchinson's time, freedom of religion
   - ☐ a. was not encouraged.
   - ☐ b. was tolerated.
   - ☐ c. was allowed only in New England.

9. Anne Hutchinson was most likely a
   - ☐ a. poor teacher.
   - ☐ b. misguided fanatic.
   - ☐ c. convincing speaker.

10. If Anne Hutchinson were alive today, it is likely that
   - ☐ a. her religious beliefs would be accepted.
   - ☐ b. she would be banished from the United States.
   - ☐ c. she would be elected to public office.

Correct Answers _____

Dry Cleaning Isn't Dry

40

Garments and other articles that are washed in liquids other than water are said to be dry-cleaned. Certain fabrics cannot withstand regular laundering and must be cleaned in this way. The dry-cleaning process is actually not dry; it is called dry because water is not used. Most modern dry-cleaning fluids are either petroleum or synthetic solvents. Different equipment is required for each of the solvents. Petroleum types can be used in open washing machines. Synthetic solvents evaporate very quickly in the air. They are used in closed, airtight washing machines.

In the dry-cleaning plant, garments and other items are first labeled with a mark or tag. Usually fabrics are examined to see if there are any badly worn or faulty areas. These might not survive the dry-cleaning process without further damage. Such areas cannot always be found by a visual inspection. Many items are measured before cleaning if the material is thought to be shrinkable. The measurements are marked on the identification tag for the guidance of the finishers.

Items for cleaning are next classified and sorted into separate portable hampers according to their fibers. Wool, silk and rayon, cotton and linen, and synthetic fibers are some of the most common classifications. The items are then further separated by colors—dark, medium, and light. Garments make up the bulk of articles that are dry-cleaned. Draperies and fine tablecloths are often dry-cleaned also.

After the articles have been sorted, they are agitated in a clear solvent and then in a soapy solvent. Next they are rinsed in a clear solution. A dry-cleaning machine using petroleum solvent contains a perforated metal cylinder, which revolves slowly in a metal shell containing the cleaning substance. The synthetic-solvent machine is sealed airtight and the cleaning fluid is then pumped into it.

Next the items are placed in an extractor. Here centrifugal force removes most of the moisture. If a petroleum solvent is used, the garments are then placed either in a drying tumbler or a drying cabinet. The tumbler consists of a rotating woven wire cylinder supported and housed within a metal casing. In addition to drying the solvent, it also deodorizes it.

The drying cabinet is used for items that cannot withstand rotary drying action, such as silk or rayon clothing. The cabinet must be properly ventilated to remove solvent gases or moisture. This is done by changing the air every few minutes.

Reading Time _____

Recalling Facts

1. The dry-cleaning process is called dry because
   - ☐ a. it is actually dry.
   - ☐ b. no water is used.
   - ☐ c. no fluids are used.

2. Modern dry-cleaning fluids include synthetic solvents and
   - ☐ a. gasoline.
   - ☐ b. bleach.
   - ☐ c. petroleum.

3. Items to be dry-cleaned are first separated according to
   - ☐ a. size.
   - ☐ b. fibers.
   - ☐ c. weight.

4. If the material is thought to be shrinkable, an item is
   - ☐ a. not able to be dry-cleaned.
   - ☐ b. measured before it is cleaned.
   - ☐ c. stretched after it is cleaned.

5. Most items cleaned are
   - ☐ a. garments.
   - ☐ b. draperies.
   - ☐ c. bed linens.

Understanding Ideas

6. You can conclude from the article that items that must be dry-cleaned
   - ☐ a. would be damaged by laundering with water.
   - ☐ b. are mostly synthetic.
   - ☐ c. can also be laundered with water.

7. It is likely that items are sorted by colors before cleaning
   - ☐ a. to prevent colors from running during the cleaning process.
   - ☐ b. to make separation after cleaning easier.
   - ☐ c. so that drying time is shortened.

8. You can conclude from the article that dry cleaning is
   - ☐ a. a relatively simple process.
   - ☐ b. a complicated process.
   - ☐ c. the most inexpensive cleaning process.

9. You can conclude from the article that rotary drying action is appropriate for
   - ☐ a. all kinds of fabrics.
   - ☐ b. delicate fabrics.
   - ☐ c. durable fabrics.

10. You can conclude from the article that solvent gases resulting from dry cleaning
   - ☐ a. are harmful to fabrics.
   - ☐ b. should not be inhaled by humans.
   - ☐ c. can be reused.

Correct Answers _____

Ethiopia

41

Located in northeastern Africa in an area known as the Horn of Africa, Ethiopia is one of the continent's largest and most populous countries. Ethiopia's landscape varies from lowlands to high plateaus. Its climate ranges from very dry to seasonally very wet. The Ethiopian population is also very mixed. There are broad differences in cultural background and traits. Methods of gaining a livelihood, languages, and religions all differ from place to place.

While occasionally occupied by other nations, Ethiopia is one of the few countries in Africa that was never truly colonized. Since World War II, Ethiopia has often been economically, politically, or militarily dependent on the major world powers. Its substantial trade deficit has been attributed to internal disorder.

The landscape of Ethiopia is dominated by central highlands of plateaus and mountains. Surrounding the highlands are hot and usually arid lowlands. The highlands are cut by deep river valleys. Situated in the tropics, Ethiopia has climatic regions that vary with elevation. Daily temperatures range seasonally from well above 100° F (40° C) in the lowlands to below freezing in the cooler upland elevations and higher.

Moisture is also unevenly distributed. Most areas have regular wet and dry periods during the year. The amount of rainfall often depends on altitude. The higher areas are wetter; the lowlands drier. At times, rains may start later or end earlier than usual. Storms may be separated by a few weeks, allowing the soil to dry out. Such drought is most common in the northern and eastern highlands and in lowland areas. When this happens, farming and herding suffer, which can lead to famine.

Ethiopia's most valuable natural resource is the soil. Although it is potentially highly productive for traditional and modern agriculture, this potential is largely unmet. In parts of Ethiopia, the soil suffers from declining fertility and erosion. The decline results from the continuous inefficient use of the soil. Farmers cultivate land that is better for grazing or land that should be left unplanted for a time. But the socioeconomic system does not reward investment in soil protection. There are also the increasing demands of a rapidly growing population. As a consequence, agricultural production per person has declined in the late 20th century.

Little has been done to find possible mineral resources in Ethiopia. Those known include gold, platinum, manganese, and salt. There is little extraction of either metallic ores or mineral fuels.

Reading Time _____

Recalling Facts

1. Ethiopia is located in
   - ☐ a. western Africa.
   - ☐ b. southern Africa.
   - ☐ c. northeastern Africa.

2. Ethiopia's most valuable natural resource is
   - ☐ a. mineral fuels.
   - ☐ b. soil.
   - ☐ c. metallic ores.

3. One cause of the decline in agricultural production per person is
   - ☐ a. famine.
   - ☐ b. decreased population.
   - ☐ c. inefficient use of soil.

4. Mineral resources in Ethiopia include gold and
   - ☐ a. salt.
   - ☐ b. soil.
   - ☐ c. silver.

5. Ethiopian people are
   - ☐ a. culturally varied.
   - ☐ b. similar in background.
   - ☐ c. very religious.

Understanding Ideas

6. From the article, you can conclude that Ethiopia is a country of
   - ☐ a. moderation.
   - ☐ b. extremes.
   - ☐ c. constancy.

7. Ethiopia could be described as
   - ☐ a. economically backward.
   - ☐ b. technologically advanced.
   - ☐ c. industrialized.

8. The article suggests that a solution to Ethiopia's problems is
   - ☐ a. increased population.
   - ☐ b. planned soil protection.
   - ☐ c. increased logging.

9. Politically, Ethiopia can be characterized as
   - ☐ a. democratic.
   - ☐ b. stable.
   - ☐ c. unstable.

10. You can conclude from the article that
    - ☐ a. there are many mineral resources in Ethiopia.
    - ☐ b. Ethiopia is a self-sufficient country.
    - ☐ c. Ethiopia cannot provide enough food to feed its growing population.

Correct Answers _____

Moths and Butterflies

42

To a poet, butterflies and moths are like fluttering flowers. Scientists call this group of insects *Lepidoptera*, a word that means "wings." The wings and certain parts of the bodies of butterflies and moths are covered with fine dust. Under a microscope, one sees that the dust is millions of scales arranged in overlapping rows. Each scale has a tiny stem that fits into a cuplike socket. The beautiful colors and markings of the insect are due to the scales, which come in a remarkable variety of colors.

Butterflies and moths look very much alike. The best way to tell them apart is to examine their antennae, or feelers. Butterfly antennae are slender, and the ends are rounded into little clubs or knobs. Moth antennae lack these knobs. Many of them look like tiny feathers, and some are threadlike.

Most butterflies fly and feed during the daytime. Moths fly at night. Butterflies rest with their wings held upright over their backs, and moths with their wings outspread. These are not safe rules to follow, however, for some moths are lovers of sunshine and some fold their wings.

Different kinds of butterflies and moths live throughout the world. They live in temperate regions, high in snowy mountains, in deserts, and in steamy jungles. They vary in size from the great Atlas moth of India, which is 10 inches (25.5 centimeters) from tip to tip of the spread wings, to the Golden Pygmy of Great Britain, which is only 1/5 inch (0.5 centimeters) across. In North America north of Mexico, there are 8,000 kinds of moths, but only 700 kinds of butterflies.

Like all insects, butterflies and moths have three pairs of legs and a body that is divided into three sections—head, thorax, and abdomen. On the middle section of the body are two pairs of wings. The pair in front is usually the larger. The scales on the wings contain a pigment that gives the insect some of its color.

Certain colors, however, and the iridescent shimmer come from the fine ridges on the scales. The ridges separate the light into the various colors of the spectrum. The beautiful blues, for example, are due to the way in which the light strikes the scales.

These insects feed on the nectar of flowers and on other plant liquids. Soon after they become adult insects, they mate, lay their eggs, and die.

Reading Time _____

Recalling Facts

1. *Lepidoptera* means
   - ☐ a. butterfly.
   - ☐ b. wings.
   - ☐ c. scales.

2. The dust on butterflies and moths is made up of
   - ☐ a. dirt particles.
   - ☐ b. feathers.
   - ☐ c. scales.

3. The best way to tell the difference between butterflies and moths is to study their
   - ☐ a. antennae.
   - ☐ b. wings.
   - ☐ c. bodies.

4. The largest moth is found in
   - ☐ a. North America.
   - ☐ b. India.
   - ☐ c. Great Britain.

5. Some of the colors on a butterfly's wings come from
   - ☐ a. a pigment contained in the scales.
   - ☐ b. the nectar of flowers.
   - ☐ c. the effect of light on moisture in the air.

Understanding Ideas

6. It is likely that a member of the *Lepidoptera* family seen flying during the day is
   - ☐ a. a butterfly.
   - ☐ b. a moth.
   - ☐ c. another kind of winged insect.

7. You can conclude from the article that butterflies and moths
   - ☐ a. prefer temperate climates.
   - ☐ b. have adapted to many different environments.
   - ☐ c. live only in dry environments.

8. The article suggests that the coloring on butterflies and moths is
   - ☐ a. likely to fade.
   - ☐ b. typical of most insects.
   - ☐ c. unusual.

9. You can conclude that the *Lepidoptera* group of insects
   - ☐ a. is completely unlike other insects.
   - ☐ b. has some characteristics in common with other insects.
   - ☐ c. is exactly like other insects.

10. You can conclude that butterflies and moths live
    - ☐ a. for many years.
    - ☐ b. longer than most insects.
    - ☐ c. only long enough to reproduce.

Correct Answers _____

Technology: Is It Art?

43

At one time, the same meaning was given to *art* that was applied to *technology*. Each was described as involving the use of skill to make or do something. Today, that blanket description is no longer true or accepted.

Technology is now generally thought of as applied science. The old definition does, however, still retain some validity. It addresses the role that skill plays in technology and in art. An artist's skill rests upon knowledge and experience; so does a technician's. The difference seems to lie in the creative application of the skill. The old definition also explains that technicians—like artists—transform matter. A sculptor may shape a block of marble into a statue. A technician may use a machine to combine silicon, metal, and plastic to produce a microchip.

Otherwise, art and technology have diverged. The goal of artists is to give permanence to the present—to speak to their age by creating works that will endure forever. The goal of technicians is to press on to the future and to new discoveries. Technology suggests permanent change and improvement. Once a new technique is developed and adopted, society does not attempt to revert to the former technique. The automobile replaced the horse and buggy; the electric light replaced kerosene lamps; sound movies replaced silent films; and word processors have made typewriters obsolete.

This forward march of technology is called progress. This type of progress does not exist in the fine arts. Today, for example, one can admire a Roman chariot, but few people would want to depend on it for transportation. By contrast, people are still astounded by the magnificence of Michelangelo's frescoes in the Vatican's Sistine Chapel. These paintings have an excellence that will never become outmoded.

In the late 20th century, art and technology have been somewhat reunited by the computer. Musical compositions can be created on a computer. It is also common to design three-dimensional models of commercial products or to sketch out blueprints using computer programs. Sculptors, filmmakers, architects, printmakers, and other workers in the visual arts increasingly use computers. It is even possible to create finished works of fine art on a computer screen. Still, the distinction between technology and art persists. Computers make the execution of some kinds of art more challenging and interesting; but they do not make the art of the present better than the art of the past.

Reading Time _____

Recalling Facts

1. The goal of technology is to
   - ☐ a. make new discoveries.
   - ☐ b. create beauty.
   - ☐ c. challenge artists.

2. Art is considered
   - ☐ a. an applied science.
   - ☐ b. a creative process.
   - ☐ c. a means to achieve progress.

3. Society regards technological changes as
   - ☐ a. advances.
   - ☐ b. negative reversals.
   - ☐ c. worthless.

4. The goal of artists is to
   - ☐ a. give permanence to the present.
   - ☐ b. make new discoveries.
   - ☐ c. outdo technology.

5. Creating musical compositions on a computer
   - ☐ a. has been possible since Michelangelo's time.
   - ☐ b. has recently been made possible.
   - ☐ c. is not possible.

Understanding Ideas

6. From the article you can conclude that Michelangelo was a great
   - ☐ a. artist.
   - ☐ b. Roman statesman.
   - ☐ c. minister.

7. Progress is a goal
   - ☐ a. for both art and technology.
   - ☐ b. more suitable to technology than to art.
   - ☐ c. more suitable to art than to technology.

8. The article suggests that computers
   - ☐ a. are useful tools for artists.
   - ☐ b. have made art more creative.
   - ☐ c. have had a negative effect on art.

9. From the article you can conclude that computers are used
   - ☐ a. primarily by technicians.
   - ☐ b. primarily by artists.
   - ☐ c. by artists and technicians alike.

10. The article wants you to understand that
   - ☐ a. technology is not art.
   - ☐ b. technology and art are the same thing.
   - ☐ c. art is impossible without technology.

Correct Answers _____

Enjoy My Hospitality

44

The sending of invitations has long played an important role in the etiquette of hospitality. Among the first people to use invitations were the North American Indians. One of their methods was to burn messages in buckskin. These were then carried by runners to all the guests. In England, in Shakespeare's time, invitations were written on large sheets of white paper and colorfully decorated. Pages or messengers carried them to the guests, who were usually required to answer. It was considered insulting to give invitations any other way. But today mailing and telephoning invitations are acceptable ways of getting guests together.

To early people, hospitality meant sharing food and shelter with friends or strangers. This has remained one of the chief ways of expressing friendship. Among the Bedouin Arabs, for example, it is considered ill-mannered and insulting to ride up to a person's tent without stopping to eat with him or her. A ceremony of hospitality among the Bedouin is the coffee-brewing ritual. The host always makes a fresh pot, using elaborate utensils that are handed down from generation to generation. Another such ritual is the tea ceremony of Japan.

A guest in Japan is given small candies and cakes, which are served on pieces of paper. To be polite, the guest must wrap any leftover food in the paper and carry it away with him or her. In the United States, too, hosts often give their guests food to take home, such as a piece of cake from a birthday party.

Many other rituals have been used to make guests feel welcome. Early Greeks gave salt to a guest as a symbol of hospitality. In Arab lands, guests must be careful not to admire a host's possessions. If they do, the host will offer the possessions to them. Among the North American Indians, smoking a tobacco pipe, the calumet, was the chief ritual of hospitality. Passing around the calumet became a feature of tribal gatherings for making peace or forging alliances.

Table manners evolved along with the development of hospitality. The ancient Greeks did not use knives, forks, or spoons for eating. They used their fingers to eat solid foods, which were cut into small pieces before being served. They drank liquids directly from cups or sopped them up with bread. The Romans did not use individual plates but took food with their fingers directly from the platters.

Reading Time _____

Recalling Facts

1. In Shakespeare's time, invitations were
   - [ ] a. sent by mail.
   - [ ] b. carried by messenger.
   - [ ] c. issued by telephone.

2. Coffee brewing is a ritual among
   - [ ] a. the Japanese.
   - [ ] b. Bedouin Arabs.
   - [ ] c. North American Indians.

3. A symbol of hospitality for early Greeks was
   - [ ] a. giving salt to a guest.
   - [ ] b. smoking a tobacco pipe.
   - [ ] c. bowing to a guest.

4. Eating utensils were
   - [ ] a. popular in early Rome.
   - [ ] b. used only by guests in early Greece and Rome.
   - [ ] c. unknown to early Greeks and Romans.

5. North American Indians smoked a peace pipe called a
   - [ ] a. calumet.
   - [ ] b. quarter.
   - [ ] c. condiment.

Understanding Ideas

6. You can conclude from the article that etiquette today is
   - [ ] a. more formal than in past times.
   - [ ] b. less formal than in past times.
   - [ ] c. nonexistent.

7. The concept of hospitality is
   - [ ] a. a new idea.
   - [ ] b. centuries old.
   - [ ] c. no longer considered important.

8. You can conclude from the article that hospitality is
   - [ ] a. mostly an issue of table manners.
   - [ ] b. delivering messages.
   - [ ] c. any way of making guests feel welcome.

9. The ritual of hospitality
   - [ ] a. is the same the world over.
   - [ ] b. varies from country to country.
   - [ ] c. always involves food.

10. In some cultures, the table manners of the ancient Greeks would be considered
    - [ ] a. refined.
    - [ ] b. courteous.
    - [ ] c. impolite.

Correct Answers _____

Remember the Alamo

45

The Alamo, an old fort in San Antonio, has been called the "Cradle of Texas Liberty." Its defense and the deaths of those who defended it inspired the cry, "Remember the Alamo!" Texas soldiers shouted this at the battle of San Jacinto, which brought Texas its independence from Mexico.

The Alamo was founded in 1718 by Spanish missionaries as the Mission San Antonio. By 1793 the mission church, later the famous fort, had fallen into disrepair and the mission was dissolved. At the time of its famous battle in 1836 the church was a roofless ruin. A high rock wall about three feet (one meter) thick enclosed an area around the church large enough to hold 1,000 men. Within that enclosure the battle of the Alamo was fought.

In December 1835 rebel Texans captured San Antonio in a significant battle. Most soldiers returned home to their families; only 80 soldiers were left to guard the city. More troops arrived later with orders to destroy the Alamo fortifications and move east with the artillery.

The Mexican commander Santa Anna was marching up through northern Mexico to regain the city. The commanding officer of the Alamo troops, Colonel William B. Travis, and Colonel James Bowie believed that the Alamo must be held to prevent Santa Anna's march into the Texas interior.

On February 22, 1836, the frontiersman Davy Crockett and 14 volunteer American riflemen arrived to help. On the same day, Santa Anna's force of almost 5,000 troops arrived. The next day, the Alamo forces and about 30 refugees withdrew into the fort and prepared for the Mexican attack. Santa Anna demanded unconditional surrender. A cannon shot from the fort came in reply. The Mexican bombardment followed.

On March 1, James Butler Bonham and a small group of volunteers arrived from nearby Gonzales to reinforce the Alamo troops. The defenders now numbered between 180 and 190.

The siege lasted 12 days. On the morning of March 6th, several thousand Mexicans stormed the fort. Every Alamo defender died. Their bodies were burned at Santa Anna's order. The only survivors were 16 women and children. Nearly 1,600 Mexicans were killed. Six weeks later, General Sam Houston led the final battle at San Jacinto. Today the Alamo is preserved as a state park. In front of the old fort is a monument to those who died there. The battle call "Remember the Alamo!" honors these heroes.

Reading Time _____

Recalling Facts

1. The Alamo was built by
   - ☐ a. Texas soldiers.
   - ☐ b. Spanish missionaries.
   - ☐ c. Mexican workers.

2. The Alamo originally served as a
   - ☐ a. jail.
   - ☐ b. fort.
   - ☐ c. mission.

3. The siege at the Alamo took place during
   - ☐ a. the battle for Texas independence from Mexico.
   - ☐ b. the Spanish-American War.
   - ☐ c. World War I.

4. Mexican troops were led by
   - ☐ a. San Antonio.
   - ☐ b. Santa Anna.
   - ☐ c. San Jacinto.

5. "Remember the Alamo" was the battle call of
   - ☐ a. Mexican freedom fighters.
   - ☐ b. Alamo invaders.
   - ☐ c. soldiers that fought in the battle of San Jacinto.

Understanding Ideas

6. At the time of the Alamo siege, the
   - ☐ a. Texans were greatly outnumbered.
   - ☐ b. Mexicans were greatly outnumbered.
   - ☐ c. Texans and Mexicans were evenly matched.

7. American volunteers helped to defend the Alamo, which suggests that
   - ☐ a. Americans believed in the cause of freedom.
   - ☐ b. Americans were hungry for battle.
   - ☐ c. Americans wanted Texas to belong to their country.

8. It is likely that soldiers inside the Alamo
   - ☐ a. thought that they would win the battle.
   - ☐ b. knew that they would be defeated.
   - ☐ c. planned to escape.

9. Calling the Alamo the "Cradle of Texas Liberty" means that
   - ☐ a. a baby was born there during the siege.
   - ☐ b. in death there is freedom.
   - ☐ c. the Alamo battle was the beginning of the Texans' fight for freedom.

10. The importance of the battle of the Alamo was that
   - ☐ a. Texas soldiers were defeated.
   - ☐ b. a battle was fought in a church institution.
   - ☐ c. it served to inspire soldiers fighting for Texas independence.

Correct Answers _____

Sink or Swim

46

Unlike many animals, humans do not swim by instinct. Yet they can learn to swim better than almost any land animal. They need only to master the proper strokes and ways of breathing.

A vital task in learning to swim is proper breathing. Swimmers inhale through the mouth and exhale through either the mouth or nose or both. Coaches often instruct pupils to inhale deeply and quickly but to exhale slowly. A swimmer can practice breathing by wading in waist-deep water, inhaling through the mouth and bending forward until the face is submerged. The swimmer then counts to 10 while holding the breath, lifts the head, and exhales. A swimmer can practice exhaling under water by keeping the eyes open and watching the bubbles. The swimmer then turns the face to one side and brings the mouth above the water to inhale.

A swimmer next learns to coast through the water. The swimmer wades into hip-deep water, faces the shore, and stoops down with arms extended beyond the head. The swimmer then shoves vigorously with the feet and floats as far as possible. To breathe, the swimmer pushes down with the hands, raises the head, and drops the feet to the bottom. A new swimmer should learn to coast 15 feet (4.5 meters) or so, exhaling under water. Swimmers who can do this are ready to learn the crawl, which is the fastest and most useful of all strokes.

When learning the crawl stroke, a swimmer floats on the stomach and kicks the legs slowly up and down. Toes should be turned inward and the knees held straight but relaxed. To move more quickly through the water, the swimmer kicks the legs in a rapid movement, called a flutter kick. The arm movement for the crawl is an alternate reaching-out stroke. The arm is fully extended directly in front of the shoulder, palm down, and then brought straight down to the hip. One arm goes forward as the other comes back.

A swimmer breathes while doing the crawl by bending forward slightly, turning the face to one side and inhaling through the mouth during the recovery of the arm on the same side. The face is then turned down and the swimmer exhales under water. A swimmer can breathe from either side, whichever is more comfortable. Most swimmers prefer to breathe to their right side during the recovery of the right arm.

Reading Time _____

Recalling Facts

1. Humans who are excellent swimmers
   - ☐ a. have mastered the proper strokes and breathing.
   - ☐ b. swim by instinct.
   - ☐ c. practice every day.

2. The fastest and most useful swimming stroke is the
   - ☐ a. back stroke.
   - ☐ b. breast stroke.
   - ☐ c. crawl.

3. The crawl requires a swimmer to float on the
   - ☐ a. back.
   - ☐ b. stomach.
   - ☐ c. side.

4. The flutter kick is a
   - ☐ a. slow arm movement.
   - ☐ b. slow leg movement.
   - ☐ c. rapid leg movement.

5. When doing the crawl, swimmers breathe from
   - ☐ a. the left side.
   - ☐ b. the right side.
   - ☐ c. either side.

Understanding Ideas

6. Proper breathing while swimming
   - ☐ a. is the same as regular breathing.
   - ☐ b. is specialized and methodical.
   - ☐ c. is not very important.

7. The flutter kick works for a swimmer much like a boat's
   - ☐ a. rudder.
   - ☐ b. oars.
   - ☐ c. wheel.

8. The arm movement for the crawl works much like a boat's
   - ☐ a. motor.
   - ☐ b. oars.
   - ☐ c. wheel.

9. The article suggests that learning to swim is best done
   - ☐ a. when a person is young.
   - ☐ b. in a pool.
   - ☐ c. in stages.

10. The article wants you to understand that
    - ☐ a. swimming is a learned skill.
    - ☐ b. some people are better swimmers than others.
    - ☐ c. swimming is an enjoyable sport.

Correct Answers _____

The Tale of Evangeline

In 1847 the poet Henry Wadsworth Longfellow published his popular poem "Evangeline." It tells of the wanderings of two French lovers who were separated during the historic fight for control of the North American continent. Their story focused on a region in the Atlantic provinces of Canada.

The French were the first Europeans to explore the St. Lawrence River and settle in Canada. To protect the entrance to the river they needed to hold the region around the Gulf of St. Lawrence, which they called Acadia. Acadia was made up of what is now New Brunswick, Nova Scotia, Prince Edward Island, and some parts of Newfoundland. In 1605 the French built a fort, Port Royal, in the region south of the gulf. Because of its geographical position, Acadia became involved in the struggle between the British and French for possession of North America. In 1621 James I of England granted Acadia to Sir William Alexander, who renamed it Nova Scotia. Time after time Port Royal was conquered by the English and retaken by the French. French families who settled in the area took no part in the wars. They also lived in peace with the friendly Micmac Indians of the region.

The final struggle for North America began in 1754. The English were in control of Acadia. English authorities demanded that unless the Acadians take an oath of allegiance to England, they would be deported. In 1755, about 6,000 Acadians were shipped to English colonies along the Atlantic coast, from Massachusetts to South Carolina. Some made their way to Louisiana to live with the French settlers there. Their descendants are called Cajuns, many of whom still speak a French dialect. The name *Cajun* derives from the English pronunciation of Acadian: "Acadjunn."

Evangeline, the heroine of Longfellow's poem, and her lover, Gabriel, lived in the village of Grand Pre in what is now Nova Scotia. On the day of their betrothal in 1755, the English summoned all the men of Grand Pre to the church. After being held prisoner for five days, they were herded onto ships. The next day Evangeline was exiled.

Evangeline spent the rest of her life wandering in search of her lover. Eventually she became a Sister of Mercy in Philadelphia, Pennsylvania. There, in an almshouse, she finally found Gabriel as he was dying. A statue of Evangeline stands today in a memorial park in Grand Pre.

Reading Time _____

Recalling Facts

1. Acadia included what is now
   - ☐ a. Massachusetts.
   - ☐ b. Nova Scotia.
   - ☐ c. Louisiana.

2. The struggle for the North American continent in that region involved
   - ☐ a. America and England.
   - ☐ b. Canada and America.
   - ☐ c. England and France.

3. Descendants of Acadians in Louisiana are called
   - ☐ a. French.
   - ☐ b. Creoles.
   - ☐ c. Cajuns.

4. The poem "Evangeline" was written by
   - ☐ a. Wordsworth.
   - ☐ b. Longfellow.
   - ☐ c. Poe.

5. Evangeline and her lover, Gabriel, were separated when
   - ☐ a. Acadians were deported by the English.
   - ☐ b. Acadians were deported by the French.
   - ☐ c. Acadians were deported by the Canadians.

Understanding Ideas

6. You can conclude from the article that Acadians took no part in wars because they
   - ☐ a. sided with the French.
   - ☐ b. sided with the English.
   - ☐ c. were peaceful people.

7. Acadians who refused to take an oath of allegiance to England showed
   - ☐ a. remorse.
   - ☐ b. pride in their heritage.
   - ☐ c. lack of courage.

8. If the English had lost the struggle for North America, it is likely that
   - ☐ a. Acadians would not have been deported.
   - ☐ b. the Micmac Indians would have revolted.
   - ☐ c. Americans would speak French.

9. The poem "Evangeline" commemorates
   - ☐ a. war.
   - ☐ b. tragic love.
   - ☐ c. revenge.

10. A statue of Evangeline was erected in Grand Pre, which suggests that
    - ☐ a. Evangeline was a real person.
    - ☐ b. England is much admired in Grand Pre.
    - ☐ c. the people of Grand Pre admire the spirit of the poem "Evangeline."

Correct Answers _____

W. Somerset Maugham

48

W┤hile studying to be a physician, W. Somerset Maugham wrote his first novel, *Liza of Lambeth*. Published in 1897, the year he completed his medical course, it is a story of life in the slums of London. The book's success determined Maugham's career. He never practiced medicine.

William Somerset Maugham was born on January 25, 1874, in Paris, France. His father was an English lawyer who was associated with the British Embassy in France. The boy's mother died when he was eight and his father when he was 10. He was brought up by a childless uncle who was a clergyman in Kent, England. By the time he went to live with his uncle, young Maugham had read many books. Maugham went to King's School in Canterbury, Kent, and then attended the University of Heidelberg in Germany. On returning to England, he entered the medical school at St. Thomas' Hospital in London.

The young author wrote rapidly but very well. He drew his material largely from the life around him. His early works include a number of successful plays, and in 1908 he had four plays running in London at the same time.

Much of Maugham's philosophy is expressed in *Of Human Bondage*, a novel based largely on his own experiences. This book, which is generally considered to be his best work, brought him recognition as a serious literary artist. It is ranked among the great novels of the twentieth century. The plot is drawn from Maugham's youth and young manhood. The literary characteristics in this book—detachment, coolness, irony, keen observation, and revelation of motives—all show his excellent craftsmanship. Among his other novels, one of the best-regarded is *The Moon and Sixpence*; Maugham patterned this book on the life of the French painter Paul Gauguin.

Maugham also wrote numerous short stories, one of the most famous being "Rain." In his short stories as well as in his novels, Maugham explains his philosophy of life. The chief elements of his philosophy are the unpredictability of human actions and reactions and one's bondage to one's emotions.

Maugham's later books include *The Razor's Edge*, a novel about a man's efforts to find peace in his soul, and *Then and Now*, a historical novel about Niccolo Machiavelli. *The Razor's Edge* and *Of Human Bondage* were adapted as motion pictures, as were some of Maugham's short stories.

Reading Time _____

Recalling Facts

1. Maugham studied
   - ☐ a. education.
   - ☐ b. medicine.
   - ☐ c. industry.

2. Maugham wrote about
   - ☐ a. the world of medicine.
   - ☐ b. the experiences of other writers.
   - ☐ c. the world around him.

3. Maugham's plays were
   - ☐ a. very successful.
   - ☐ b. failures.
   - ☐ c. seen on Broadway.

4. Maugham's best work is generally considered to be
   - ☐ a. *Of Human Bondage.*
   - ☐ b. an untitled book of philosophy.
   - ☐ c. *The Moon and Sixpence.*

5. Maugham wrote
   - ☐ a. magazine articles, novels, and movies.
   - ☐ b. medical journals.
   - ☐ c. novels, plays, and short stories.

Understanding Ideas

6. According to the article, Maugham should be considered
   - ☐ a. the greatest novelist of all time.
   - ☐ b. one of the greatest novelists of the 20th century.
   - ☐ c. a mediocre writer.

7. Maugham considered a person's emotions
   - ☐ a. a great blessing.
   - ☐ b. more important than intellect.
   - ☐ c. the source of many problems.

8. The article suggests that an important element in good writing is
   - ☐ a. portrayal of unpredictable emotions.
   - ☐ b. the ability to write from personal experience.
   - ☐ c. excellent craftsmanship.

9. Maugham believed that people respond to circumstances
   - ☐ a. in predictable ways.
   - ☐ b. in unpredictable ways.
   - ☐ c. by avoiding conflict.

10. Maugham was primarily a writer of
    - ☐ a. nonfiction.
    - ☐ b. fiction.
    - ☐ c. autobiography.

Correct Answers _____

Human Disease

49

A disease is a condition that impairs the proper function of the body or of one of its parts. Every living thing, both plants and animals, can yield to disease. People, for example, are often infected by tiny bacteria. And bacteria, in turn, can be infected by even smaller viruses.

There are hundreds of different diseases. Each has its own particular set of symptoms or signs. These are clues that enable a doctor to diagnose the problem. A symptom is something a patient can detect, such as fever, bleeding, or pain. A sign is something a doctor can detect, such as a swollen blood vessel or an enlarged internal body organ.

Every disease has a cause. However, the causes of some diseases remain to be discovered. Every disease also displays a cycle of beginning, course, and end, when it disappears or it partially disables or kills its victim.

Infectious diseases can be transmitted in many ways. They can be spread in droplets through the air when infected persons sneeze or cough. Whoever inhales the droplets can become infected. Some diseases can be passed through contaminated eating or drinking utensils. Once an infectious organism gains a foothold in the body, it begins to thrive and multiply. Its progress may be slow or fast, depending upon the nature of the pathogen. The symptoms of the common cold appear within a few days of infection. But the symptoms of kuru, an uncommon disease of the nervous system, often appear three years or longer after infection.

Every infectious disease has an incubation period. This is the length of time between the pathogen's gaining a foothold in the body and the appearance of the first symptoms of the disease. Several factors also determine whether a person will become the victim of a disease after being infected. The number of invading germs in the dose of the infection influences the outbreak of disease. So does the virulence of the pathogens; that is, their power to do harm. In addition, the condition of the body's immunological defenses also affects the probability of catching a disease.

Many infectious diseases are contagious; that is, they can easily be passed between people. To acquire certain contagious diseases, someone need only be in the presence of someone with the disease, come in contact with an infected part of the body, or eat or drink from contaminated utensils.

Reading Time _____

Recalling Facts

1. Disease strikes
   - ☐ a. mostly plants.
   - ☐ b. mostly animals.
   - ☐ c. both plants and animals.

2. Pain is
   - ☐ a. the cause of a disease.
   - ☐ b. an infection.
   - ☐ c. a symptom of a problem.

3. The symptoms of a cold appear
   - ☐ a. seconds after infection.
   - ☐ b. within a few days of infection.
   - ☐ c. weeks after infection.

4. The time between infection and the appearance of the first symptoms of a disease is the
   - ☐ a. incubation period.
   - ☐ b. contagious period.
   - ☐ c. cycle period.

5. Contagious diseases are
   - ☐ a. difficult to pass between people.
   - ☐ b. easily passed between people.
   - ☐ c. never passed between people.

Understanding Ideas

6. A person who is weak and undernourished is
   - ☐ a. more likely to yield to disease.
   - ☐ b. less likely to yield to disease.
   - ☐ c. neither more nor less likely to yield to disease.

7. A doctor's ability to detect a disease is dependent on
   - ☐ a. the cause of the disease.
   - ☐ b. the skill of the doctor.
   - ☐ c. a disease's incubation period.

8. One way to avoid a disease is to
   - ☐ a. avoid people who are infected with the disease.
   - ☐ b. avoid seeing a doctor.
   - ☐ c. understand the symptoms of the disease.

9. Diseases are caused by
   - ☐ a. impaired body function.
   - ☐ b. excessive bleeding.
   - ☐ c. bacteria and viruses.

10. You can conclude from the article that a disease with a long incubation period
    - ☐ a. has a better chance of spreading infection.
    - ☐ b. has a lesser chance of spreading infection.
    - ☐ c. will most likely prove harmless.

Correct Answers _____

Planet Earth

Each planet, including Earth, travels around the Sun in a regular orbit. Ancient astronomers thought that the orbits of the planets were circular. It is now known that the orbits are elliptical, though the orbits of some planets are almost circular. The extent to which Earth departs from a perfectly circular path is very slight. The orbits of Mercury and Mars are the most eccentric of the planets.

The planets nearest to the Sun move faster than do those farther away. Mercury, the closest, orbits the Sun in about three months. Neptune, the most distant planet, takes 164 years to make one trip around the Sun.

To people on Earth, the planet seems steady and immovable. Because it gives no sensation of motion, it is hard to realize how rapidly it moves through space in its orbit around the Sun. Earth takes a whole year to make one round trip, which seems rather slow. On the average, however, it moves at 18.5 miles (29.8 kilometers) per second, or 66,600 miles (107,226 kilometers) per hour.

While Earth and the other planets move around the Sun, the Sun itself moves through a galaxy, or large group of stars, called the Milky Way. The Milky Way is a collection of about one hundred billion stars. They are arranged in a disk-like shape with a bulge at the center. This central bulge contains about three-quarters of all the stars in the galaxy.

No one has made exact measurements of the Milky Way. Scientists, however, can see other galaxies in the sky. By comparing what they see with what they know about the Milky Way, they can make rough guesses about its size and shape and the number of stars it contains.

The entire Milky Way galaxy seems to be slowly rotating. The stars near the center probably move around the hub faster than those near the edge, just as the planets nearest to the Sun move faster than do those farther away. The Sun is about two-thirds of the way out from the center of the galaxy. Astronomers estimate that the Sun with its planets takes about 200 million years to make one trip around the Milky Way.

The Milky Way galaxy is part of a cluster of galaxies known as the Local Group. This group consists of a total of 17 galaxies.

Reading Time _____

Recalling Facts

1. The orbits of the planets around the Sun can best be described as
   - ☐ a. circular.
   - ☐ b. elliptical.
   - ☐ c. eccentric.

2. How quickly a planet orbits the Sun depends on the
   - ☐ a. size of the planet.
   - ☐ b. planet's distance from the Sun.
   - ☐ c. shape of its orbit.

3. The speed of Earth as it revolves around the Sun is nearly
   - ☐ a. equal to the speed of light.
   - ☐ b. 7,000 miles (11,270 kilometers) per hour.
   - ☐ c. 70,000 miles (112,700 kilometers) per hour.

4. A galaxy is a
   - ☐ a. system of planets.
   - ☐ b. large group of stars.
   - ☐ c. cluster of orbits.

5. The Milky Way appears to be
   - ☐ a. moving further into space.
   - ☐ b. slowly rotating.
   - ☐ c. the largest galaxy.

Understanding Ideas

6. Presuming that all galaxies have the same number of stars, you can conclude from the article that the Local Group consists of
   - ☐ a. about the same number of stars in the Milky Way.
   - ☐ b. about 17 times the number of stars in the Milky Way.
   - ☐ c. half the number of stars in the Milky Way.

7. You can conclude from the article that the science of astronomy
   - ☐ a. is growing as knowledge is gained.
   - ☐ b. is vastly uniformed about the Milky Way.
   - ☐ c. has reached its limits.

8. The Sun's location in the Milky Way means that it is
   - ☐ a. clustered with most of the other stars in the galaxy.
   - ☐ b. located away from most of the stars in the galaxy.
   - ☐ c. moving into another galaxy.

9. In the time it takes the Sun to make one trip around the Milky Way, Earth will have completed about
   - ☐ a. 100 million orbits around the Sun.
   - ☐ b. 200 million orbits around the Sun.
   - ☐ c. 300 million orbits around the Sun.

10. Since the Sun is about two-thirds of the way out from the center of the Milky Way, you can conclude that
    - ☐ a. it is the fastest moving star in the galaxy.
    - ☐ b. most other stars move faster.
    - ☐ c. most other stars move slower.

Correct Answers _____

Put 'Em Up!

51

The sport of boxing is the art of attack and defense with the fists. Some people feel that boxing is too violent and dangerous and should be abolished. It has, however, endured in one form or another since ancient times and has a devoted following.

Boxing matches take place in a ring. The ring is a square platform (often called the squared circle), padded and covered with canvas. It ranges from 16 to 20 square (4.9 to 6 meters) feet in professional contests and from 12 to 20 square (4 to 6 meters) feet in amateur contests. Multiple lengths of rope attached to posts in each corner enclose the ring. Each fighter has his own corner, diagonally across from his opponent's. The other two corners are neutral.

If a fighter falls or is knocked down, he must get to his feet within 10 seconds. The referee counts seconds aloud as long as the fighter remains down. If the referee reaches the number 10, he declares a knockout (KO). Sometimes a fighter is hopelessly beaten without being counted out. The referee then awards the bout to his opponent on a technical knockout (TKO).

The bout is decided on points if neither contestant has suffered a knockout or a technical knockout or has been disqualified by a foul. Points are scored for the number of blows landed, for a clever defense, and for aggressiveness. The decision is reached by a majority vote of the judges on the basis of total points scored.

A good offense is built around four classes of punches—jab, straight blow, hook or cross, and uppercut. The jab is a sharp, light punch delivered by straightening out the bent arm. It can be used effectively to harass an opponent and keep him off-balance. A straight punch may carry the weight of the body behind it and will result in a knockout if landed in a vital spot. The hook or cross, either left or right, is a swinging blow, aimed to slip by the opponent's guard. The uppercut is a blow directed upward, usually aimed at the jaw or the midsection.

Clever moves are also useful to a boxer. Feinting is bluffing with one hand before delivering a blow with the other. Leading is opening an attack, usually with a left jab. Countering is throwing a hard punch at the opponent at the exact moment he leads off.

Reading Time _____

Recalling Facts

1. The ring where boxing matches take place is often called the
   - ☐ a. canvas.
   - ☐ b. squared circle.
   - ☐ c. corner.

2. A technical knockout is when a fighter
   - ☐ a. is knocked out.
   - ☐ b. is beaten without being counted out.
   - ☐ c. remains down after ten seconds.

3. If neither contestant is knocked out, the winner is picked
   - ☐ a. by the audience.
   - ☐ b. by the referee.
   - ☐ c. on the basis of total points scored.

4. The punch that is directed upward is called the
   - ☐ a. jab.
   - ☐ b. straight punch.
   - ☐ c. uppercut.

5. Bluffing with one hand before delivering a blow with the other is called
   - ☐ a. leading.
   - ☐ b. countering.
   - ☐ c. feinting.

Understanding Ideas

6. From the article you can conclude that boxing has endured because
   - ☐ a. supporters of the sport outnumber its opponents.
   - ☐ b. opponents of the sport outnumber its supporters.
   - ☐ c. the sport has received good publicity.

7. Judges are important in boxing because they
   - ☐ a. control the type of fighting.
   - ☐ b. make sure no one is hurt.
   - ☐ c. can choose the winner.

8. People who are against boxing are fearful that
   - ☐ a. boxers will get hurt.
   - ☐ b. people in the audience will get hurt.
   - ☐ c. the sport will lose money.

9. Boxing is different from other sports in that
   - ☐ a. the opponents are usually men.
   - ☐ b. one opponent tries to physically harm another.
   - ☐ c. the smartest person wins.

10. From the article you can conclude that the purpose of a technical knockout is to
    - ☐ a. shorten the length of a match.
    - ☐ b. prevent a losing boxer from being seriously hurt.
    - ☐ c. encourage good sportsmanship.

Correct Answers _____

The "Iron Horse"

52

The "iron horse" that pulls railroad passenger or freight cars is a power plant on wheels, complete in itself. The term *locomotive* is used for this type of power plant only when it can be uncoupled from the rail cars. Some power plants are part of a passenger car. They may be self-propelled rail-diesel cars. Others could be streamlined electric trains. The term *locomotive* is not used to refer to these power plants.

Until the 1950s, the steam engine locomotive ruled supreme. In North America, Europe, and much of the rest of the world, the steam locomotive has since been replaced by the diesel-electric locomotive. In areas of high rail traffic, as along the East Coast of the United States and in Central Europe, many rail lines have been electrified and use electric locomotives. Today, steam engines are used only in countries, such as China, where coal is much cheaper or more readily available than oil.

Many large locomotives actually develop enough power to supply a small city. Most of the time, however, only a small fraction of this power is needed to pull a train. Once it is underway, a train needs only a few pounds of pulling power to keep one ton of its weight in motion. Full power is needed at first to start the train and then to pull it up a steep grade. To start a long train, the locomotive first backs up to loosen the couplings between cars. In this way, one car after the other begins moving forward. A long string of tightly coupled rail cars cannot be moved all at once.

The old steam locomotive is driven by a steam engine. Steam from the boiler is fed to the engine's cylinders to move pistons back and forth. Connecting rods from the pistons then move the driving wheels. The firebox at the rear end of the boiler is fed with coal or oil. In a large locomotive, the coal or oil is stored in a tender, or a separate, attached rail car. The tender also holds the water that is turned into steam. The exhaust from the steam cylinders is directed up the smokestack to create a heavy draft for the boiler fire. The discharge of the used steam from the cylinders is controlled by valves. The stop-and-go release of the steam up the stack makes the noise that is called the locomotive's puffing.

Reading Time _____

Recalling Facts

1. An "iron horse"
   - ☐ a. pulls railroad passenger or freight cars.
   - ☐ b. produces electricity for railroad cars.
   - ☐ c. provides steam for railroad cars.

2. The term *locomotive* refers to a power plant that
   - ☐ a. is a part of a railroad passenger car.
   - ☐ b. can be uncoupled from railroad cars.
   - ☐ c. is a self-propelled passenger car.

3. To keep one ton of a train's weight in motion, a locomotive must supply
   - ☐ a. full power.
   - ☐ b. an equal amount of pulling power.
   - ☐ c. a few pounds of pulling power.

4. A locomotive's puffing sound comes from
   - ☐ a. wheel action on railroad tracks.
   - ☐ b. pistons moving back and forth.
   - ☐ c. the stop-and-go release of steam up the smokestack.

5. Until the 1950s, most locomotives were driven by
   - ☐ a. electricity.
   - ☐ b. steam.
   - ☐ c. diesel fuel.

Understanding Ideas

6. You can conclude from the article that steam engine locomotives are probably
   - ☐ a. easier to run than diesel-electric locomotives.
   - ☐ b. less efficient than diesel-electric locomotives.
   - ☐ c. making a comeback.

7. The article suggests that railroad transportation is
   - ☐ a. losing its popularity.
   - ☐ b. popular around the world.
   - ☐ c. more popular than any other kind of transportation.

8. You can conclude that the danger of fire is
   - ☐ a. less likely with electric locomotives.
   - ☐ b. more likely with electric locomotives.
   - ☐ c. completely eliminated with electric locomotives.

9. It is likely that in China steam engines will
   - ☐ a. continue to be used for some time.
   - ☐ b. be replaced by electric locomotives.
   - ☐ c. become more expensive to run than engines requiring oil.

10. You can conclude that the power produced by locomotives
    - ☐ a. should be greatly reduced to save energy.
    - ☐ b. is greater than is needed most of the time.
    - ☐ c. is inadequate to drive trains efficiently.

Correct Answers _____

The Mighty Plant

53

Wherever there is sunlight, air, and soil, plants can be found. On the northernmost coast of Greenland, the Arctic poppy peeps out from beneath the ice. Mosses and tussock grasses grow in Antarctica. Flowers of vivid colors and great variety force their way up through the snow on mountainsides. Many shrubs and cacti thrive in deserts that go without rain for years at a time. Rivers, lakes, and swamps are filled with water plants. There are few places on the earth where plants have not been known to grow.

Botanists, scientists who study plants, have named and described nearly 500,000 different kinds of plants. They estimate that another 500,000 undiscovered species exist in less explored ecosystems such as tropical forests. In addition, about 2,000 new plants are discovered or developed every year.

Human beings are completely dependent upon plants. Directly or indirectly, plants provide the food, clothing, fuel, shelter, and other necessities of life. People's direct dependence on crops such as wheat and corn is obvious. These crops are used to make many food products including breads and pastas. But without grass and grain, the livestock that provide people with food and other animal products could not survive either.

The food that plants store for their own growth is also the food that humans and other organisms need. In North America, the chief food plants are cereal grains such as corn, wheat, oats, rice, barley, rye, and buckwheat. Legumes are the second greatest source of food from plants. Legumes such as peas, beans, soybeans, and peanuts are high in protein and oil. Sago, taro, and cassava are major starchy foods for people in certain tropical places. Seaweeds are an important part of the diet in some cultures, especially in Asia.

Most seasonings are derived from plant materials. People have used herbs and spices for centuries to flavor and preserve food. Some seasonings, such as pepper and nutmeg, are obtained from dried fruits. Others, including thyme, sage, and rosemary, come from leaves. Plant stems provide such spices as ginger and cinnamon.

Most beverages also come from plants. Coffee and tea are prepared by steeping plant parts in hot water. Other drinks are made by nature: orange, lemon, and grape juice; coconut milk; apple cider; and apricot nectar are examples. Some beverages come from processed plants. For example, cola drinks are made from the kola nut of tropical America.

Reading Time _____

Recalling Facts

1. Scientists have named
   - ☐ a. 100 different kinds of plants.
   - ☐ b. 2,000 different kinds of plants.
   - ☐ c. 500,000 different kinds of plants.

2. The chief food plants in North America are
   - ☐ a. seasonings.
   - ☐ b. cereal grains.
   - ☐ c. legumes.

3. Legumes include
   - ☐ a. wheat and rice.
   - ☐ b. peas and peanuts.
   - ☐ c. thyme and sage.

4. Cola drinks are made from
   - ☐ a. the kola nut.
   - ☐ b. cocoa.
   - ☐ c. coconuts.

5. Coffee and tea are prepared by
   - ☐ a. baking plants.
   - ☐ b. grinding the roots of plants.
   - ☐ c. steeping plant parts in hot water.

Understanding Ideas

6. You can conclude from the article that human beings
   - ☐ a. could not survive without plants.
   - ☐ b. need plants to breathe.
   - ☐ c. are discovering new plants every day.

7. The article wants you to understand that plants
   - ☐ a. indirectly provide people with animal products.
   - ☐ b. are not as important as animals.
   - ☐ c. are by-products of animals.

8. You can conclude that places where plants do not grow
   - ☐ a. are very rainy.
   - ☐ b. lack sunlight, air, or soil.
   - ☐ c. are cold.

9. You can conclude that the diets of people in different cultures depend on
   - ☐ a. the types of plants grown locally.
   - ☐ b. crop rotation.
   - ☐ c. scientists.

10. The article suggests that as new plants are discovered,
    - ☐ a. familiar plants will become less useful.
    - ☐ b. new plants will take the place of old plants.
    - ☐ c. there is tremendous potential for expanding people's knowledge of plants.

Correct Answers _____

Learning to Act

54

I magine a person with all of the desires, fears, thoughts, and actions that compose the personality of a man or a woman. Acting is becoming that imaginary person. Whether the character, or role, that the actor creates is based on someone who really lived, a playwright's concept, or a legendary being, that creation comes to life through the art of acting. Acting is an ability to react, to respond to imaginary situations and feelings. The purpose of this ancient profession, one of the world's oldest, is, as Shakespeare has Hamlet say, "to hold, as 'twere, the mirror up to Nature, to show...the very age and body of the Time, his form and pressure."

It is the audience that sees itself in the mirror of acting. Acting is a process of two-way communication between actor and audience. The reflection may be realistic, as the audience sees its own social behavior. The reflection may be a funny or critical exaggeration. Or the audience may see a picture of the way it thinks or a fantastic projection of the way it feels.

Acting makes use of two kinds of physical skills: movement and voice. Either may dominate. Body movement is highly developed in Far Eastern acting traditions, while the voice has ruled in Western cultures. If either voice or movement takes over completely, the activity is usually not called acting but dance, perhaps, or singing. But neither ballerinas nor operatic singers can reach the top of their professions without acting.

In one sense, there is no technique of acting. When the actor is on the stage or in front of a camera, there should be no thought of technique. The actor attempts simply to be there. Technique in acting has to do with getting ready to act. There are two basic requirements: developing the necessary physical external skills and freeing the internal emotional life. The physical skills needed by actors have been understood since ancient times. They are a well-developed body and voice. They include the ability to imitate other people's gestures and mannerisms. In addition, actors need to master the physical or vocal abilities required by the type of theater.

Before the 20th century, the inner emotional training of actors was not thought about in a systematic way. Young actors developed by watching older, more experienced performers. The creation of emotional truth on stage was largely thought of as a problem of imitation.

Reading Time _____

Recalling Facts

1. Acting is a process of two-way communication between
   - ☐ a. actor and director.
   - ☐ b. actor and audience.
   - ☐ c. actors.

2. Acting makes use of two kinds of physical skills:
   - ☐ a. movement and voice.
   - ☐ b. singing and dancing.
   - ☐ c. listening and speaking.

3. In addition to developing the necessary physical external skills, actors must
   - ☐ a. study other actors.
   - ☐ b. free the internal emotional life.
   - ☐ c. take acting lessons.

4. Acting is the ability to
   - ☐ a. project the voice.
   - ☐ b. exaggerate.
   - ☐ c. react.

5. Before the 20th century, young actors developed by
   - ☐ a. watching more experienced performers.
   - ☐ b. reading different types of plays.
   - ☐ c. living life to the fullest.

Understanding Ideas

6. The aspect of a theater most likely to influence an actor's technique is
   - ☐ a. location.
   - ☐ b. size.
   - ☐ c. age.

7. An actor in front of a camera rather than on a stage would probably need to
   - ☐ a. become more dramatic in voice and movement.
   - ☐ b. become less dramatic in voice and movement.
   - ☐ c. react in the same way.

8. The main difference between acting now and before the 20th century was an emphasis on
   - ☐ a. imitation rather than freed emotion.
   - ☐ b. movement rather than voice.
   - ☐ c. voice rather than movement.

9. Acting can be thought of as
   - ☐ a. a reflection of the thoughts, feelings, and actions of the actors.
   - ☐ b. a reflection of the thoughts, feelings, and actions of the audience.
   - ☐ c. a writer's interpretation of life.

10. You can conclude from the article that the most successful actors are those who
    - ☐ a. have the most experience.
    - ☐ b. study the hardest.
    - ☐ c. do not appear to be acting.

Correct Answers _____

Unit 3

Reading Rate

Instructions: Put an X on the line above each lesson number to show your reading time and words-per-minute rate for that lesson.

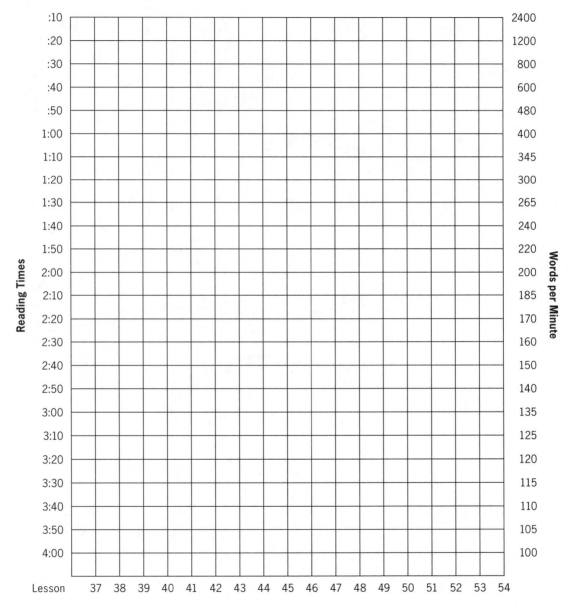

Reading Times		Words per Minute
:10		2400
:20		1200
:30		800
:40		600
:50		480
1:00		400
1:10		345
1:20		300
1:30		265
1:40		240
1:50		220
2:00		200
2:10		185
2:20		170
2:30		160
2:40		150
2:50		140
3:00		135
3:10		125
3:20		120
3:30		115
3:40		110
3:50		105
4:00		100

Lesson   37 38 39 40 41 42 43 44 45 46 47 48 49 50 51 52 53 54

Unit 3

Comprehension Score

Instructions: Put an X on the line above each lesson number to indicate your total correct answers and comprehension score for that lesson.

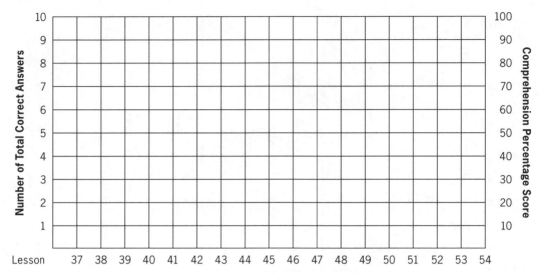

Answer Key Unit 1

1: Birds of the Air
1. a
2. b
3. b
4. c
5. c
6. a
7. c
8. c
9. b
10. b

2: Sleeping Through the Winter
1. b
2. a
3. b
4. a
5. b
6. c
7. c
8. b
9. c
10. c

3: Swim Safely
1. a
2. b
3. c
4. b
5. a
6. b
7. a
8. c
9. a
10. a

4: Bows and Arrows
1. c
2. b
3. a
4. a
5. b
6. c
7. b
8. a
9. c
10. a

5: Life of a Logger
1. b
2. c
3. b
4. a
5. c
6. c
7. b
8. a
9. b
10. a

6: The Need for Clean Water
1. b
2. c
3. c
4. a
5. c
6. b
7. a
8. a
9. c
10. b

7: Whitney's Cotton Gin
1. b
2. c
3. c
4. b
5. b
6. c
7. b
8. a
9. c
10. a

8: Written by Hand
1. b
2. c
3. a
4. c
5. a
6. c
7. b
8. b
9. c
10. a

9: Easier Living with Inventions
1. a
2. b
3. a
4. c
5. b
6. a
7. b
8. c
9. b
10. c

Answer Key Unit 1 *continued*

10: Lighter Than Air
1. c
2. c
3. a
4. b
5. b
6. b
7. b
8. c
9. a
10. a

11: Early Egypt
1. b
2. c
3. b
4. c
5. b
6. a
7. b
8. c
9. a
10. a

12: John Paul Jones
1. b
2. c
3. a
4. b
5. c
6. c
7. b
8. b
9. a
10. c

13: Problem Drinking
1. b
2. c
3. a
4. b
5. c
6. b
7. c
8. b
9. b
10. b

14: Rabbits and Hares
1. b
2. b
3. a
4. c
5. b
6. a
7. c
8. a
9. b
10. c

15: Save the Watershed
1. c
2. b
3. a
4. b
5. a
6. b
7. c
8. a
9. c
10. a

16: The Acropolis
1. b
2. b
3. c
4. a
5. b
6. c
7. c
8. b
9. c
10. b

17: The Cowpuncher's Partner
1. b
2. c
3. b
4. b
5. a
6. a
7. b
8. c
9. b
10. a

18: Try Jogging for Fitness
1. b
2. b
3. c
4. a
5. c
6. b
7. c
8. a
9. c
10. b

Answer Key Unit 2

19: The Birthplace of Human Beings

1. b
2. c
3. a
4. a
5. b
6. c
7. b
8. a
9. c
10. c

20: Thomas Jefferson

1. c
2. b
3. b
4. c
5. c
6. a
7. a
8. b
9. a
10. c

21: Early Weapons and Defenses

1. a
2. c
3. c
4. a
5. c
6. b
7. b
8. c
9. a
10. b

22: He Wrote *Robinson Crusoe*

1. c
2. a
3. c
4. a
5. b
6. c
7. c
8. b
9. a
10. a

23: The Earliest Writing

1. a
2. b
3. a
4. c
5. a
6. b
7. c
8. a
9. c
10. a

24: An Ancient Empire

1. a
2. c
3. c
4. b
5. a
6. b
7. a
8. b
9. b
10. c

25: The Great Whales

1. a
2. b
3. b
4. c
5. c
6. b
7. a
8. c
9. c
10. a

26: The Making of a Jet

1. b
2. c
3. c
4. b
5. c
6. b
7. b
8. a
9. a
10. a

27: Gators and Crocs

1. a
2. b
3. b
4. c
5. b
6. c
7. c
8. a
9. a
10. b

Answer Key Unit 2 *continued*

28: How Clothing Is Made
1. b
2. b
3. a
4. c
5. c
6. c
7. a
8. b
9. a
10. b

29: Paints
1. a
2. b
3. c
4. a
5. a
6. a
7. b
8. b
9. b
10. b

30: Early Civilization
1. b
2. b
3. a
4. b
5. c
6. c
7. c
8. b
9. b
10. a

31: Ships of the Desert
1. a
2. a
3. c
4. b
5. b
6. c
7. c
8. b
9. b
10. a

32: Sicily
1. a
2. b
3. c
4. c
5. a
6. b
7. c
8. b
9. b
10. a

33: The Start of Language
1. b
2. a
3. c
4. c
5. b
6. b
7. b
8. b
9. a
10. c

34: Alpine Life
1. b
2. c
3. c
4. a
5. b
6. b
7. b
8. a
9. a
10. c

35: Crabs
1. b
2. b
3. c
4. b
5. c
6. a
7. b
8. a
9. c
10. a

36: The Worst of Pests
1. b
2. b
3. c
4. b
5. a
6. a
7. b
8. a
9. a
10. b

Answer Key Unit 3

37: At Home in the Zoo
1. b
2. b
3. a
4. a
5. c
6. a
7. b
8. b
9. b
10. c

38: Fire Extinguishers
1. a
2. c
3. b
4. c
5. b
6. b
7. b
8. a
9. c
10. c

39: Anne Hutchinson, Religious Pioneer
1. b
2. c
3. b
4. a
5. c
6. b
7. a
8. a
9. c
10. a

40: Dry Cleaning Isn't Dry
1. b
2. c
3. b
4. b
5. a
6. a
7. a
8. b
9. c
10. b

41: Ethiopia
1. c
2. b
3. c
4. a
5. a
6. b
7. a
8. b
9. c
10. c

42: Moths and Butterflies
1. b
2. c
3. a
4. b
5. a
6. a
7. b
8. c
9. b
10. c

43: Technology: Is it Art?
1. a
2. b
3. a
4. a
5. b
6. a
7. b
8. a
9. c
10. a

44: Enjoy My Hospitality
1. b
2. b
3. a
4. c
5. a
6. b
7. b
8. c
9. b
10. c

45: Remember the Alamo
1. b
2. c
3. a
4. b
5. c
6. a
7. a
8. b
9. c
10. c

Answer Key Unit 3 *continued*

46: Sink or Swim
1. a
2. c
3. b
4. c
5. c
6. b
7. a
8. b
9. c
10. a

47: The Tale of Evangeline
1. b
2. c
3. c
4. b
5. a
6. c
7. b
8. a
9. b
10. c

48: W. Somerset Maugham
1. b
2. c
3. a
4. a
5. c
6. b
7. c
8. c
9. b
10. b

49: Human Disease
1. c
2. c
3. b
4. a
5. b
6. a
7. b
8. a
9. c
10. a

50: Planet Earth
1. b
2. b
3. c
4. b
5. b
6. b
7. a
8. b
9. b
10. b

51: Put 'Em Up!
1. b
2. b
3. c
4. c
5. c
6. a
7. c
8. a
9. b
10. b

52: The "Iron Horse"
1. a
2. b
3. c
4. c
5. b
6. b
7. b
8. a
9. a
10. b

53: The Mighty Plant
1. c
2. b
3. b
4. a
5. c
6. a
7. a
8. b
9. a
10. c

54: Learning to Act
1. b
2. a
3. b
4. c
5. a
6. b
7. b
8. a
9. a
10. c